Archaeological
Adventures
in the
Outer Hebrides

Archaeological
Adventures
in the
Outer Hebrides

GERALD PONTING

LIVING HISTORY

THE ISLANDS BOOK TRUST
URRAS LEABHRAICHEAN NAN EILEAN

First published in 2025 by The Islands Book Trust,
Kinloch Community Hub, Balallan, Isle of Lewis, HS2 9PN

www.islandsbooktrust.org

Designed and Typeset by
Palimpsest Book Production Ltd, Falkirk, Stirlingshire

A CIP catalogue record for this title is available from the British Library.

Printed by Gomer Press Ltd, Llandysul, Wales

ISBN: 978-1-917834-00-1

OSCR
Scottish Charity Regulator
www.oscr.org.uk
Registered Charity
SC032682

Scottish Charity Regulator
Registered Charity SC032682

Eoropie

Adabrock

Borve, Lewis

Barvas

Dalmore

Carloway

Gress

Kneep

Newmarket

Shulishader

STORNOWAY

CALLANISH

LEWIS

Sandwick

Achmore

Ballalan

North Harris hills

Pairc hills

Borve, Harris

Northton

TARBERT

HARRIS

Ensay

Outline map of Lewis and Harris, showing locations
of sites mentioned in the text

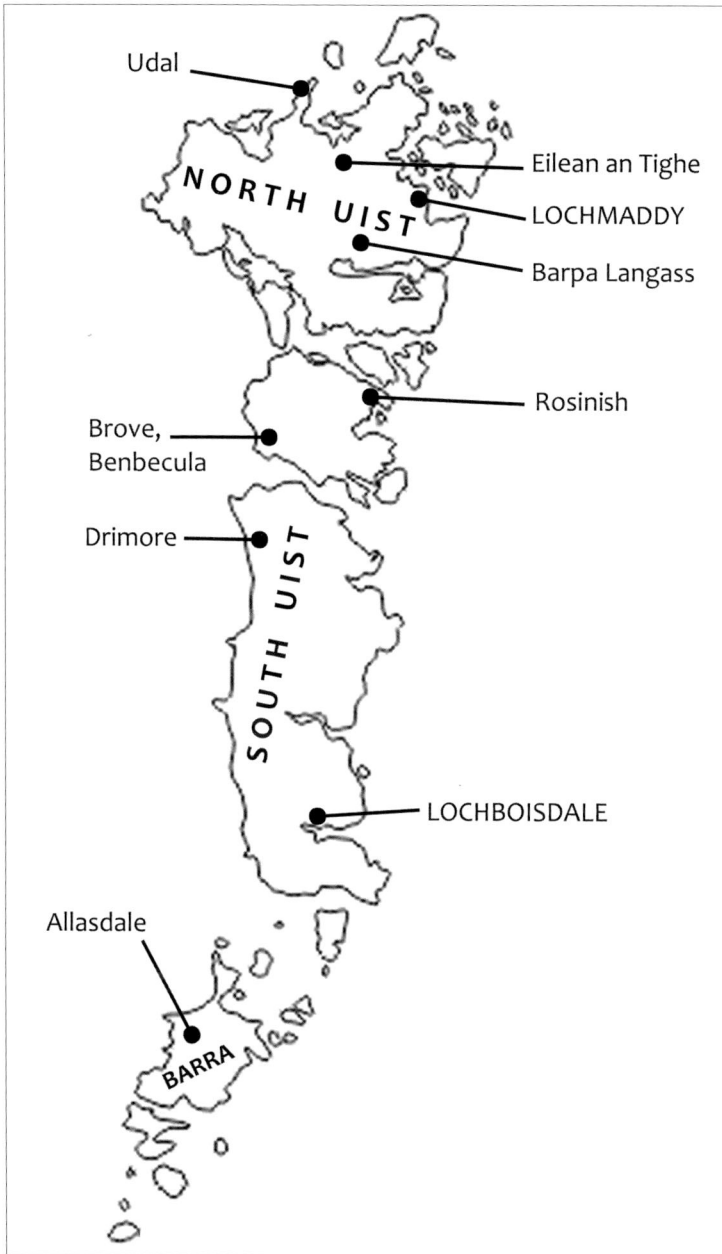

Outline map of the Uists, Benbecula and Barra,
showing locations of sites mentioned in the text

Contents

Part 4 – Finds and excavations, 1891 – 1974

CONTENTS

Part 5 – Finds and Excavations, 1975-1984

Part 6 – Elsewhere and Afterwards

CONTENTS

Foreword

It is a great honour to have been asked to provide this Foreword to the aptly named *Archaeological Adventures in the Outer Hebrides*. The book is a cracking read, and it demonstrates what a huge contribution Gerald has made to the prehistoric archaeology of the Outer Hebrides – not just through his diligent research and fieldwork, but also by raising public awareness of the richness of the archaeological record in this part of Scotland, and by campaigning for improved facilities for exploring, managing and displaying it.

Few people can fail to be impressed by the majesty of the complex megalithic monument at Calanais, and Gerald and his first wife Margaret were duly wowed when they holidayed in Lewis in 1970. However, as he explains, he had no idea then of the major role this monument was to play in their lives.

Most visitors come, admire the stones, take photographs and leave with happy memories. What Gerald went on to do with Margaret, in the decade after moving to Lewis in 1974 to take up his teaching position at the Nicolson Institute, was different and truly remarkable. Not only did they make a thorough study of past research, travelling down to the National Archives in Kew to examine Pitt Rivers' 1885 field notebooks from his visit to Calanais, for example, they also fruitfully explored the monument itself. They were able to demonstrate that Stone 35 is not in its original location; they rediscovered the lost Stone 33A in the East Row and were instrumental in getting it re-erected; and through a combination of dogged determination and serendipity, they located the knocked-off tip of Stone 19 and were again instrumental in getting it refitted.

Moreover, they published the first guidebook to Calanais (among many other publications), and they publicised the awe-inspiring spectacle of the Major Southern Lunar Standstill when, for several months every 18.6 years and as viewed from the north end of the Avenue, the moon skims the horizon, shaped like a supine woman, then disappears before shining in the circle as it sets.

All this work was duly recognised when they became finalists in the 1978 British Archaeological Awards, receiving a presentation from Prince Charles (as he was then) as runners-up in the Legal and General Award for Initiative. Their foray into the world of archaeoastronomy also led to appearances at major conferences and a lecture tour in America.

Gerald's work at Calanais was only part of his huge contribution to the prehistoric archaeology of the Outer Hebrides, and his various adventures and endeavours are described most entertainingly in this volume. It is Gerald we have to thank for encouraging finders of artefacts to report and take care of their finds, using his regular column in the *Stornoway Gazette* as an effective way of raising awareness.

Had it not been for his exhortation to keep waterlogged finds wet and report them promptly, the magnificent haft of the c. 5200-year-old Shulishader axe – a star exhibit not just in the permanent displays of the National Museum of Scotland but also in the recent exhibition, *The World of Stonehenge*, at the British Museum – would have become a shrivelled mess.

The *Stornoway Gazette* column also captured precious nuggets of information about other finds that are otherwise so easily lost to a wider world, and likewise served to let local readers know about important finds (such as the Late Bronze Age Adabrock hoard, and the Dell swords) that are housed off-island and had been published in the *Proceedings of the Society of Antiquaries of Scotland*, a journal not widely read in the Outer Hebrides (although now freely available online).

Gerald's work demonstrates how vital it is to bridge the gap between 'academic' and professional archaeology, on the one hand, and the local communities among whom the artefacts and monuments have been found, on the other.

It is fitting that this engaging account of Gerald's archaeological adventures in the Outer Hebrides is being published during the current Major Southern Lunar Standstill season, and when the new and greatly improved Calanais Visitor Centre is being constructed, ready for its opening in 2026. I am so glad that Gerald accepted my suggestion of putting down his experiences in writing; we are all the beneficiaries from his wit, wisdom and sheer hard work.

Dr Alison Sheridan
FBA FRSE FSA FSA Scot ACIFA,
Vice President of *Archaeology Scotland* and
Board member of Urras nan Tursachan

PART 1

Introduction

———

CHAPTER 1

TREASURE TROVE!

Murdo Macinnes, cutting his peats at Dell on the Isle of Lewis in 1891, made a very unusual discovery – a complete bronze sword, almost two feet long, its blade still sharp after 3000 years.

Nineteen years later and about three miles to the northwest at Adabrock, Donald Murray also discovered Bronze Age treasure when cutting peat - axeheads, glass and gold beads, together with various tools and fragments of a large bronze bowl.

Declared Treasure Trove, these items went on display in the National Museum of Antiquities in Edinburgh, as the 'Aird Dell Sword' and the 'Adabrock Hoard'. Like so many island treasures, most notably the famous Lewis Chessmen, walrus-ivory pieces found at Uig in 1831, they were destined to remain on the mainland.

The Aird Dell Sword and the Adabrock Hoard, loaned by NMS for display in Ness. The hoard includes eleven bronze items - axeheads, spear-head, hammer-head, razors and fragments of a bowl – also whetstones and beads. More details of these items are given in chapter 28.
Image by kind permission of National Museums Scotland.

However, in 2023 National Museums Scotland loaned the sword and the hoard for display at Comunn Eachdraidh Nis, the community museum in Ness. After over a hundred years, residents could see these iconic local artefacts without a visit to Edinburgh.

Any *information* about ancient finds was generally available only in academic libraries, with little or no details diffused back to those who lived near the find spot. For instance, a detailed report on the Adabrock Hoard appeared in 1914 in the *Proceedings of the Society of Antiquaries of Scotland**.

In one of my earliest archaeology columns, in the Stornoway Gazette

---

* To this day, PSAS is the primary journal for Scottish archaeological discoveries – and now entirely and freely available online.

of March 1983, I summarised the Adabrock report from nearly 70 years previously (chapter 28). Like the return of the treasure to Ness, one of my aims was to make such 'lost' information available locally.

Some chapters of this book, notably in Part 4, are also revised versions of my Gazette articles, updated where possible. Other chapters relate to fascinating experiences told from a personal point of view, and in some cases previously unpublished.

CHAPTER 2

WE WERE LEWIS INCOMERS

I lived on the Isle of Lewis from 1974 to 1984 before returning to southern England, initially to the village in rural Hampshire where I had lived as a boy.

My father had a small farm with a herd of dairy cows, and operated a milk round in our village. During the Second World War, he was a member of the local Home Guard. After my years at the small village school, I attended the boys' grammar school in Salisbury. I graduated with a degree in Zoology at the University of Southampton, then trained as a teacher at the University of Leicester.

I met my first wife, Margaret, when we were both student volunteers on a conservation work-camp in Anglesey. She had been brought up in the West Midlands. We married and settled in Suffolk, both in teaching posts, and enjoyed camping holidays in Austria, in Turkey and on Crete. A fascinating summer month in Iceland in 1965 was seen as an unusual, even a rash, choice but we loved the remoteness.

This may have influenced us when choosing to holiday in the Outer Hebrides in 1970. We explored from Ness to Castlebay in a motorcaravan with our first child. As tourists, we visited the Callanish Stones, with no thought that they would come to play a major part in our lives.

We returned to the Hebrides, now with two small children, for the next four summer holidays. We spent most of our time on the Uists, based at Scolpaig Farm (now, unbelievably, the site of a spaceport). But during our 1974 holiday, we took the ferry to Tarbert and drove to Stornoway, where I accepted a teaching post at the Nicolson Institute, the island's large and prestigious secondary school. We also agreed the purchase of a house near Callanish.

So it was that, just before Christmas 1974, we left Suffolk and, as our English friends saw it, *emigrated to some incredibly remote island in the far north-west*. After a crossing of the Minch delayed by stormy weather, we were welcomed by our new neighbours and settled in.

I joined the Biology staff at the Nicolson, while five-year-old Benjamin enrolled at Breasclete Primary School, a short walk from our home. Once Rebecca also started school, Margaret took up a post as part-time peripatetic music teacher to several schools on the West Side.

Moving to our new island home, it had been our intention to become partially self-sufficient. We cut peats for fuel and cultivated a plot to grow vegetables. We kept chickens and goats for eggs, milk and, occasionally, meat. We sometimes fished for mackerel from an inflatable that was little more than a toy. Pet lambs were a must for the children in their first spring. Rebecca's 'Prickle' grew into a lusty ram, well-known at fanks for answering to the call of a small girl. We made hay for the goats and sheep. We also had a cat or two, as well as pet rabbits and guinea pigs.

We became inured to the wind and the rain; and were seen to respect the Lewis Sabbath. On sunny Sundays we went to a beach, Dalbeg and Dalmore being favourites, or for walks on the moors, or wildlife watching on the cliffs. Fascinating events occurred in Stornoway, including the visit of a replica Viking ship and of a French nuclear submarine. Our late Queen came to open the new council offices; and we celebrated her Silver Jubilee. Our ewe Silver had a lamb in 1997, which of course had to be named Jubilee.

Becoming amateur archaeologists was never part of the plan, but ......

CHAPTER 3

HOW WE BECAME THOUGHT OF AS 'THE ISLAND'S ARCHAEOLOGISTS'

Loch Erisort Woollens' store in Cromwell Street was also, surprisingly, Stornoway's only bookshop. In 1975, for Margaret's 34th birthday, I bought a copy of Professor Alexander Thom's *'Megalithic Sites in Britain'*. Little did I realise that this would change our lives. During our eleven years living in Suffolk, our interest in archaeology had been limited to watching Magnus Magnusson's regular *Chronicle* documentaries on BBC TV, and visiting heritage sites.

Moving to Lewis, our new home was just over a mile from a major prehistoric site, but we found a dearth of local information about the Callanish Stones. Thom's book devoted several pages to the site. More significantly, his bibliography listed other sources of information, going

Discussing the Stones on a winter's day.

5

back to 1703. We tracked down these sources and found others, mostly through correspondence with Edinburgh museums, archives and libraries. Soon we had acquired enough knowledge to self-publish the first-ever guidebook to 'The Standing Stones of Callanish'.

Documentary studies of Callanish led to on-site discoveries. It became something of an obsession to search for previously unrecorded megaliths in the district. After submitting an account of our research, we were presented with one of the British Archaeological Awards 1978 and achieved our own spot on *Chronicle*. This, of course, became a local news story.

In 1977, a house builder in Eoropie had found stone features when digging foundations. The *Stornoway Gazette* ran a story about our assistance in excavating a probable Iron Age dwelling. I was interviewed on local radio about this and other discoveries. Our status as the local experts on ancient objects was emphasised when two workmen rang our doorbell to show us 'a stone tractor seat' that they had found.

Subsequently, we received visits and phone calls about stone axeheads, a ball of fat in a peat bank, a Viking skull and so on; as well as social visits from professors and megalith enthusiasts from around the world. Our motto became *'There's no such thing as on ordinary week'.* My archaeology

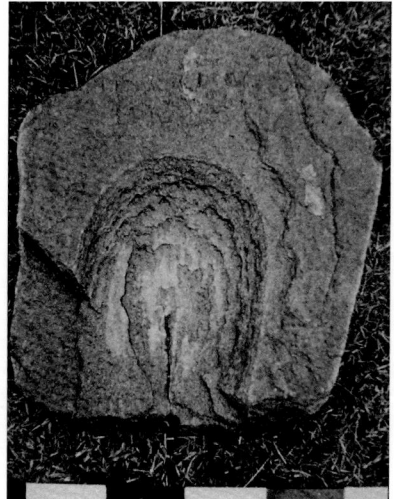

A saddle quern, similar to the one compared to a 'tractor seat'. Scale shows 10 cm markings.

column, which appeared most weeks in the *Gazette* in 1983-4, further enhanced my profile.

> *Originally conceived to bring together some of those articles, this book has expanded beyond that. Not intended as an academic work, it is a personal memoir with my own recall and diary entries backed up by paperwork and photographs that have survived the decades.*
>
> *Readers should be aware that, throughout this book, when I use the words 'we' or 'our', I am referring to studies carried out jointly with Margaret from 1975 onwards. After I returned to Hampshire in 1984, Margaret stayed on Lewis and continued her researches, but I had little continuing contact with island archaeology.*
>
> *Where they are relevant to the topic of a chapter, I have added summaries of later studies. However, there are sure to be other archaeological discoveries, or differing opinions, of which I am unaware.*

PART 2

Archaeological Background

CHAPTER 4

'HOW OLD IS IT?'

Early antiquaries had no means of dating ancient artefacts, other than as 'pre-Roman'. In the 1830s Christian Thomsen, Director of the National Museum of Denmark, proposed a 'Three Age' system of Stone Age, Bronze Age and Iron Age.

Thomsen's system, with subdivisions, continues to be used by today's archaeologists. The Old Stone Age (Palaeolithic) does not concern us in the Hebrides. The Middle Stone Age (Mesolithic) lasted from around 9000 BC to 4000 BC. The New Stone Age (Neolithic) ended in 2500 BC, when the short copper-using Chalcolithic period began, followed by the Bronze Age from c. 2200 BC. The division between the Bronze Age and the Iron Age is around 800 BC in Scotland. Bronze and Iron Ages are each divided into Early, Middle and Late by specialists.

Daniel Wilson used the ages of Stone, Bronze and Iron for sections in his 1851 book, *'Prehistoric Annals of Scotland**. This title was the first use of the word 'prehistoric' in English, though 'préhistorique' had been used in French at least eighteen years earlier. In England, the end of (unwritten) prehistory and the start of (written) history is clearly defined by the Roman invasion of AD 43. In regions of Scotland largely unaffected by Roman settlement, the division is less clear.

When the Society of Antiquaries of Scotland, founded in 1780, moved to new premises in 1843, it reorganised its extensive collection of artefacts according to the Three Age system. Eight years later, the Government agreed to take ownership of the Society's collections and to fund better premises for their display. The new National Museum of Antiquities of Scotland was opened on Princes Street in 1859. There was increased interest in Scottish antiquities in the 1840s and 1850s including investigations of the Callanish Stones.

Jens Jacob Worsaae, excavating sites in Denmark, was one of the first to develop a scientific approach to archaeology, stressing the importance of stratigraphy. Finds needed to be recorded layer by layer, as *the deeper you dig, the older it is'*. At most sites, the *relative* age of a stratigraphic layer could be established by examining sherds of pottery found within it.

While objects made of wood, leather or even metal rarely survive from the past, fired clay remains undamaged in most soils, perhaps as tiny fragments - potsherds. Just as styles of dress in a photographic portrait can enable a fashion expert to date the image, so a distinctively shaped or decorated potsherd can enable an archaeologist to pin it to a particular prehistoric culture.

As an example, the characteristic shape and decoration of their pottery gave a name to the 'Beaker People' of the Chalcolithic and Early Bronze

---

* Daniel Wilson left Scotland two years after the publication of his important book. He had a long and distinguished career as a Professor of History in Toronto. I mentioned this in my column, but the version printed in the Gazette included a typo. It read that Wilson visited Scotland 'only once more, in 1978'. Correcting this the following week, I commented – 'Not many men manage to revisit their homelands at the age of 162!'.

Age. Many sherds of their pottery were found in the sandy layers which we excavated at Dalmore.

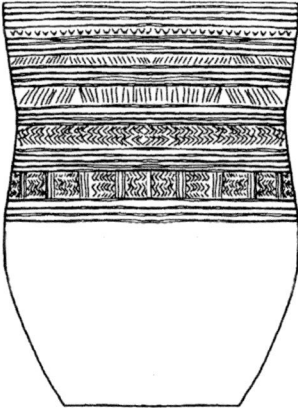

An idealised drawing
of a Beaker, showing
ornate decoration

A sherd of Beaker
pottery found at Dalmore
(chapters 44, 45)

Giving an *actual* date for an archaeological layer, rather than a relative one from pottery finds, was normally impossible until Willard Libby's research in Chicago. He was awarded the Nobel Prize for Chemistry in 1960 for his discovery of the radioactive isotope carbon-14. Remarkably, he also found an archaeological use for the discovery – radiocarbon dating.

Without going into scientific detail, carbon-14 exists in tiny amounts in all plants and animals, but after death the amount remaining decreases at a fixed rate. Measuring the amount of C-14 remaining in a piece of bone can establish the date of the creature's death – and thus the age of the layer where the bone was found. Such results are inevitably approximate, and give a range of possible dates. Where a large enough piece of wood survives, dendrochronology (tree ring dating) can fix a date more precisely.

Patrick Ashmore, Ancient Monuments Inspector responsible for the Callanish Stones, devoted 24 pages of his excavation report (chapter 7) to radiocarbon dating results. Perhaps his most interesting conclusion is that the most likely date for the building of the central stone circle was *somewhere in the time span 2950 to 2650 BC*. This is roughly contemporary with the first stones at Stonehenge but significantly earlier than the erection of the great sarsen trilithons.

CHAPTER 5

PEAT GROWTH CREATES AN ARCHIVE FOR ARCHAEOLOGY

Most of the interior of the Isle of Lewis is blanketed with around two metres of peat. The rate of peat formation increased when the climate became damper around the start of the Iron Age. Waterlogged soil contains few air spaces and the bacteria which cause decay cannot live. Dead vegetation fails to decompose completely, accumulating in the form of peat … at a rate of a millimetre or more per year. Other organic materials within the peat also fail to decay, so wood and pollen are preserved for thousands of years. The preservation of pollen grains provides a particularly useful 'archive' (chapter 41).

Although peat-cutting for domestic fuel is less widely practised today, during my time on Lewis the peats neatly stacked outside the house were still the main source of heating for most families. 'Cutting the peats' was an important communal early-summer activity. From the archaeological point of view, this meant that the general public sometimes made important discoveries, simply because they were exposing earlier levels.

At the lowest levels, prehistoric artefacts might be found, such as the axe haft dated to very approximately 3000 BC (chapter 40). The middle levels might reveal less ancient items, for example the bog butter from around AD 1100 (chapter 51).

A 1970s peat bank near Breasclete

Taking a global view, peat is the largest carbon sink, storing more carbon even than the world's forests. Burning peat as a fuel, or using it in horticulture, releases carbon dioxide and makes its contribution to climate change.

In May 1983, I wrote an article about ancient wooden artefacts from commercial peat cuttings in Somerset. Archaeologists had a watching brief on finds, which included the remains of an ornately decorated longbow, a ladle, a mallet and a food bowl, all good evidence for the quality of prehistoric woodworking. Each wooden item was kept moist and rapidly transferred to laboratories for conservation. Left exposed to the air, they would have shrivelled and lost shape quite rapidly.

My article was titled *'LOOK OUT WHEN YOU ARE CUTTING THE PEATS'* and I ended with this paragraph: *'Could I suggest to all peat cutters that they look more closely at any wood they find among the peat this year. If it appears to be shaped in any way, even if it looks merely like a branch sharpened at one end, I'm sure the Edinburgh laboratories would be interested. Surround any find with damp peat, wrap it in polythene and get in touch with the Gazette as soon as possible. Financial rewards are not guaranteed.'*

Several months earlier (January 1983), the *Gazette* editor had noted - *'It is worth mentioning that Mr Ponting predicted early last year that following the reward to the Balallan boy who found axeheads, "there could be other rewards forthcoming for eagle-eyed peat cutters in the spring". His predictions came true with the reward to the Point family who found an axe and handle in their peak bank.'* (See chapter 40.)

CHAPTER 6

RECORDING SITES IN THE 1920s AND THE 2020s

The Western Isles are rich in archaeological remains. Some are well known with a considerable volume of writings about them. Others are totally obscure and of interest only to specialists. But between these two categories of sites, there are some that are little known, despite being clearly visible to the casual observer. Two large dilapidated prehistoric cairns near Coll and Gress are good examples.

'The Inventory'

Though largely superseded today by online databases, much information about such sites can be found in a book published almost a hundred years ago. Although commonly called *'The Inventory'*, the full title page reads: *'The Royal Commission on Ancient and Historical Monuments and Conservations of Scotland, Ninth Report with Inventory of Monuments and Constructions in the Outer Hebrides, Skye and the Small Isles. Edinburgh. 1928'*.

The 230-page book, with many photographs, includes 473 monuments between North Rona and Barra Head, 203 on Skye and 15 on Canna, Eigg, Muck and Rhum. It is, of course, out of print and fetches high prices at antiquarian book-sellers.

The Ancient Monuments Act of 1885 had protected only a few of the most important monuments, and by 1905 there were complaints of its inadequacy to protect the large numbers of other sites. As a result, a Royal Commission was appointed for Scotland in 1908, with the remit to list all ancient monuments in the country – it was commonly referred to as RCAHMS.

The Scottish Commissioners took two early decisions which became the foundation of its work. An inventory would be produced county by county; and all monuments would be examined by Commission staff before inclusion. For four months in the autumn of 1909, Dr Alexander Curle cycled around Berwickshire, visiting sites. The resultant small booklet was considered too superficial. Succeeding volumes, it was decided, needed to be more detailed and more comprehensive.

Surveying for Skye and the Western Isles began in 1914; interrupted by the First World War, it was completed in 1925. Almost all of the sites were visited by Dr J Graham Callender, who later became director of the National Museum. He suffered difficulties in reaching some sites as weather '... *in these regions is at once an influential and an unstable factor. The fact that so many ancient monuments exist on islets in lochs also imposed peculiar limitations. In some cases, a partially submerged causeway could be used, though only at the cost of a wetting; very rarely a boat was available...*'. His superiors congratulated Callender for his *'skill, care and unflagging energy'*.

The Inventory contained the only measured plans for many sites and these are remarkably accurate considering the conditions under which they were surveyed. Returning to the chambered cairns near Coll and Gress, we find that Dunan near Coll was recorded as *'much disturbed'*. Another entry describes Carn a' Mharc, a larger but equally despoiled cairn nearly two miles northwest of Gress Lodge. Two small circular groups of stones nearby were *'doubtless the remains of shielings'*, the ancient cairn having been considered a convenient quarry. Much more detail about chambered tombs throughout Scotland was given in two volumes by Audrey Henshall (1963 and 1972).

Priests Glen Stone Circle

This is the Inventory entry for Priests Glen.

> Stone circle (remains), Priests Glen, Laxdale. Three prostrate stones mark the periphery of this circle, which is about 50 yds in diameter. One, on the N. arc is 5 ft long and 3 ft 2 ins broad: the others, on the S. arc, 30 ft 6 ins apart, are 5 ft and 5 ft 6 ins long and 2 ft 8 ins and 2 ft 5 ins broad respectively.

I attempted an update, assisted by a group of pupils from the Nicolson Institute. Friday afternoon class timetables were replaced by 'Activities', a chance for teachers to share their hobbies with pupils who had, or aspired to, a similar interest. I usually offered a Photography Activity, but sometimes instead offered Archaeology, including visits to Callanish and to Achmore.

At least twice, we visited the stones at Priest's Glen near Newvalley, about two miles from the school. With about eight pupils, of varying ages, we took measurements and probed for additional stones. Back at school, during another session, we must have drawn up a plan. Sadly I can find no paperwork in my surviving files, so my only record is this, which I submitted to *'Discovery and Excavation in Scotland'* in 1981 –

PRIEST'S GLEN (Stornoway p) G Ponting
Stone circle
NB 409 354 Survey of four known prone slabs, followed by probing along a postulated perimeter, suggested the existence of 4 further prone stones beneath the turf, forming a circle of approximately 47m diameter.
NICOLSON INSTITUTE ARCHAEOLOGY GROUP

'Discovery and Excavation in Scotland'

This annual publication is a means of keeping up with what other archaeologists have discovered. Any discovery ranks a record in *'DES'* — anything from the casual find of a single medieval coin to a major excavation. Archaeologists can briefly outline their site-work with a delay measured only in months after completion; this is especially valuable when full publication often suffers major delays – see next chapter. Submissions to *DES* are now made online and previous issues have been digitised for easy online access.

CHAPTER 7

DELAYS IN EXCAVATION REPORTS

After a few weeks, or months, or even several seasons, the excavation is finished. The trenches are filled in, the tools are stored, the workers have gone their separate ways. The finds are bagged and labelled; photographs, drawings and daily notes are all carefully filed. But the work of the Director continues, for months or more likely for years, as he or she arranges research by appropriate specialists.

- Identifying the distinctive shapes and styles of decoration of pottery, usually fragmentary, may identify the period in which it was made.
- The detailed examination of animal bones produces information on the varieties of domestic animals that were kept or hunted and thus the diet of the people.
- Bones shaped into tools may suggest crafts practised.
- Pollen analysis identifies the vegetation that grew around the site - perhaps including crops.

- Radiocarbon techniques produce dates for bone, wood, charcoal, etc
- Lithics experts study prehistoric arrowheads, axeheads and scrapers. They are able to build up a picture of the ancient technology that produced the tools.
- Geological examination of stone may identify its source, thus helping to establish a pattern of trade routes.
- The list of experts to be consulted in 'post-excavation' work could go on and on.

In due course the Director receives all of the technical reports, which may form appendices longer than his or her own account, based on records kept at the time. The sheer volume of information meant that, in the past, archaeological journals often lacked the space required. With the coming of the internet, this problem was largely solved.

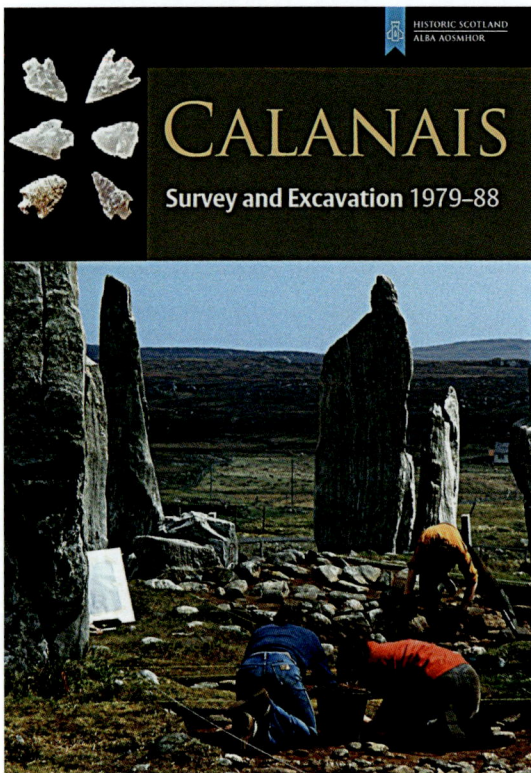

Patrick Ashmore's report on his excavations at Callanish in 1980 and 1981 became freely available on the website of Historic Environment Scotland in 2016. It runs to no less than 1241 pages and includes, as Patrick himself admitted, *sometimes bewildering detail*. With admirable dedication, he had spent 4500 hours of his retirement bringing all of the information together.

A delay of 30 years between excavation and publication is by no means unusual. The various experts and the Director all have other calls on their time in their universities, museums or other institutions. However carefully the excavation was budgeted, financial constraints can occur in the post-excavation work.

In the case of Lindsay Scott's dig on North Uist in 1937, Derek Simpson's seasons on Harris in 1966 and 1967 and Iain Crawford extensive work at the Udal from 1963 to 1984, it fell to other authors to publish more detailed accounts after the directors' deaths.

And why is so much detail necessary? Sometimes, total re-appraisal of an old, but important, excavation may be needed, decades after the original report was published. New archaeological knowledge can be applied only if *all* the facts have been recorded. Also, authors were not always careful to separate their subjective opinions from objective facts. A good example is the report on Scott's work at Eilean an Tighe on North Uist (chapter 43).

CHAPTER 8

SOME THINGS ARE STUCK IN THE PAST

This book is, in a sense, stuck in a time warp. Writing in the 2020s about events that happened – or which I first studied – in the 1970s and 1980s, there is always a conflict between the way things were then and the way they are now. This has effects in four main areas – place names, local government, archaeological bodies, and measurements.

Placenames

I apologise to all my Gaelic-speaking readers for retaining the English spellings of village names, those that were familiar to me in the 1980s, before Gaelic spellings started to appear on road signs. Many errors would certainly have crept in, had I tried to use the Gaelic names.

I continue to refer to the stones as 'Callanish', as I believe that this is familiar to a wider audience than 'Calanais'. Formerly written 'Classerness' or 'Callernish', the name was probably derived not from Gaelic but from Old Norse *Kallarðarness*, meaning a 'promontory from which a ferry is called'. Before there was a bridge to Great Bernera, the island was reached by ferry from Callanish Pier.

The Gaelic spelling Calanais, introduced by the Ordnance Survey in the 1990s, has been adopted by Historic Environment Scotland, which cares for the stones, and by Urras nan Tursachan (the Standing Stones Trust), which operates the Visitor Centre.

Names of smaller localities are generally given in Gaelic, particularly

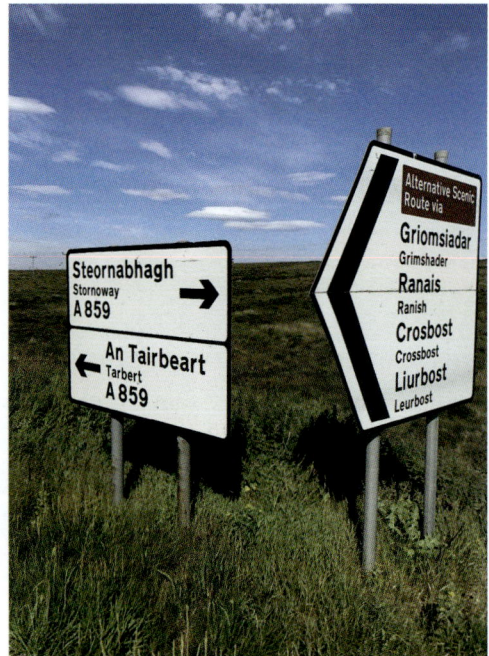

Gaelic is the mother tongue of many people in the Western Isles. Bilingual road signs have become general since the time that I lived on Lewis.

as used by their excavators. I have usually given English translations, such as 'the underground house' for Tigh Talamhanta on the Isle of Barra. My apologies if any of these seem inaccurate; I've usually relied on earlier writers.

Administration

When I was first appointed to a teaching post in Stornoway, my employer was *Ross and Cromarty County Council*, based in Dingwall on the mainland. Just a few months later, with local government reorganisation, the *Western Isles Islands Council* took responsibility from the Butt of Lewis to Barra Head. It used the Gaelic name *Comhairle nan Eilean* (Council of the Islands), later changing it to *Comhairle nan Eilean Siar* (Council of the Western Isles).

Archaeological Bodies

Organisations change their names and status over the years. In the 1970s and 1980s, we had many dealings with the *National Museum of Antiquities of Scotland*. Amalgamated with the *Royal Scottish Museum*, it is now part of the institution known as *National Museums Scotland*, with objects displayed in the *National Museum of Scotland* on Chambers Street, Edinburgh. So when I refer to the 'National Museum' in other chapters, I mean whichever entity was active at the time concerned.

In Victorian times and later, ancient monuments were the responsibility of the *Office of Works*. We always dealt with SDD (AM) – the *Ancient Monuments* section of the *Scottish Development Department* – including its *Central Excavation Unit*. Later, *Historic Scotland* took on the role.

The *Royal Commission on Ancient and Historical Monuments of Scotland* – RCAHMS – acted as a collector of information from 1908 onwards. Its archive, the *National Monuments Record of Scotland* (NMRS) provided many sources which were useful in our research. It is now called the *National Record of the Historic Environment* (NRHE).

In 2015, HS and RCAHMS combined to form *Historic Environment*

Scotland (HES). It maintained an online catalogue of Scotland's archaeology and buildings, known as *Canmore*. As this book goes to press, the data are being incorporated into a new website, *trove.scot*.

Measurements

Today, all archaeological dimensions are recorded in metric units, from millimetres to kilometres. But one does not have to go back too far to find inches, feet, yards and miles as the usual units. There is a mixture in this book, as I have chosen to keep units as they were expressed at the time, mainly because conversion produces illusions of accuracy.

As an example, a measurement of 10 feet, perhaps not intended to be precisely 10 feet and no inches, converts to an apparently accurate 3.048 metres. Conversely, 10 metres becomes 32 feet 9.6 inches.

Eras

For dates, I have chosen to retain the long-established BC / AD notation, rather than BCE / CE which is less familiar to non-historians.

Academic Status

My apologies to academics whose research I have quoted, if I have omitted (or been unaware of) their status as Doctor or Professor, titles which anyway may change over time. In addition, researchers may move between institutions during their careers.

PART 3

Studying the Megaliths

———

While we became involved in other aspects of island archaeology, our main focus was always the Standing Stones of Callanish (Tursachan Calanais) and related megaliths.

CHAPTER 9

A CHRONOLOGY OF CALLANISH STUDIES – to 1974

City dwellers visiting Lewis soon become aware of the impact that the dome of the sky makes on their senses. Most of us live in places where buildings, even trees, block out the awareness of the heavens. Prehistoric peoples probably saw no great distinction between landscape and skyscape as the environment in which they lived. **Archaeoastronomy** is the study of ancient Man's relationship with the sun, moon and stars*.

For much of the 18th, 19th and early 20th centuries, the popular perception was that Stonehenge and other stone circles were built and used by the druids. From the 1960s onwards, thanks to publicity for archaeoastronomical theories, notably those of Gerald Hawkins and Alexander Thom, a different idea became entrenched in the public mind – prehistoric peoples were avid sky watchers and perhaps worshippers of the sun and moon.

Outlining a chronology of Callanish studies in this chapter and continuing in chapter 26, it becomes clear that this concept gradually became central to the public perception of Callanish.

55 BC   Diodorus of Sicily wrote about Hyperborea, an island in the far north, where there was a 'spherical' temple, where the moon seemed very close to the earth, and where the god visited every nineteen years. Earlier, Eratosthenes had described the Hyperborean temple as 'winged'. Along with other authors, I think it very likely that both were referring to a distant knowledge of Callanish. Spherical and winged could refer to the circle with east and west rows, while the 'moon-god' near the horizon every nineteen years ties in well with our southern moon skim theory (chapter 19).

c.1680   The Callanish Stones were first mentioned in print, though not named. John Morisone wrote of Lewis, *'in several places there are great stones standing up straight in ranks'*.

1703   Martin Martin suggested that the *'Chief Druid'* had addressed the people from the great centre stone.

1808   James Headrick, a hundred years ahead of his time, claimed that Callanish was a *'rude astronomical observatory'* where priests *'could*

---

* The discipline was at first called 'astro-archaeology', but this was dropped as it seemed to imply excavations among the stars! The current term 'cultural astronomy' also includes study of the practices of present-day indigenous peoples.

mark out the rising of the sun, moon and stars, the seasons of the year, even of the hours and divisions of the day'.

1824   John MacCulloch published a plan of Callanish showing several stones as 'fallen',

1825   It is probable that Callanish villagers started cutting peats among the stones of the avenue around this time.

1846   Jacob Worsaae, visiting from Denmark, made sketches in his field notebook, the earliest known illustrations of the site.

1854   A paper by Henry Callender included an engraving of the stones, showing local people extracting peat near the circle. He proposed that the peat should be cleared to find whether *any building had been erected at the original level'*.

1857   Peat was cleared from around the stones of the Callanish circle, revealing the cairn at the centre. This resulted in a flurry of interest over the next few years, many antiquaries visiting to make their own notes, plans or drawings.

1858   Peat was cleared from around the stones at circles Callanish II, III and IV.

1885   Pitt Rivers visited Callanish in his role as Inspector of Ancient Monuments, with the result that the stones were placed in government Guardianship (see next chapter).

1909   Norman Lockyer, Astronomer Royal, published *'Stonehenge and other British Stone Monuments Astronomically Considered'*. Without having visited Callanish he claimed to have found two 'star lines'.

1912   Rear Admiral Boyle T Somerville first suggested an alignment with the moon. His survey of Callanish was the most accurate to date and introduced the numbering of individual stones that we still use today.

1939   The Stones were transferred from Guardianship to state ownership.

1965   Gerald Hawkins, a British-born professor of astronomy in America, published *'Stonehenge Decoded'*, a book which became an international best-seller. His theories, uniquely for those days

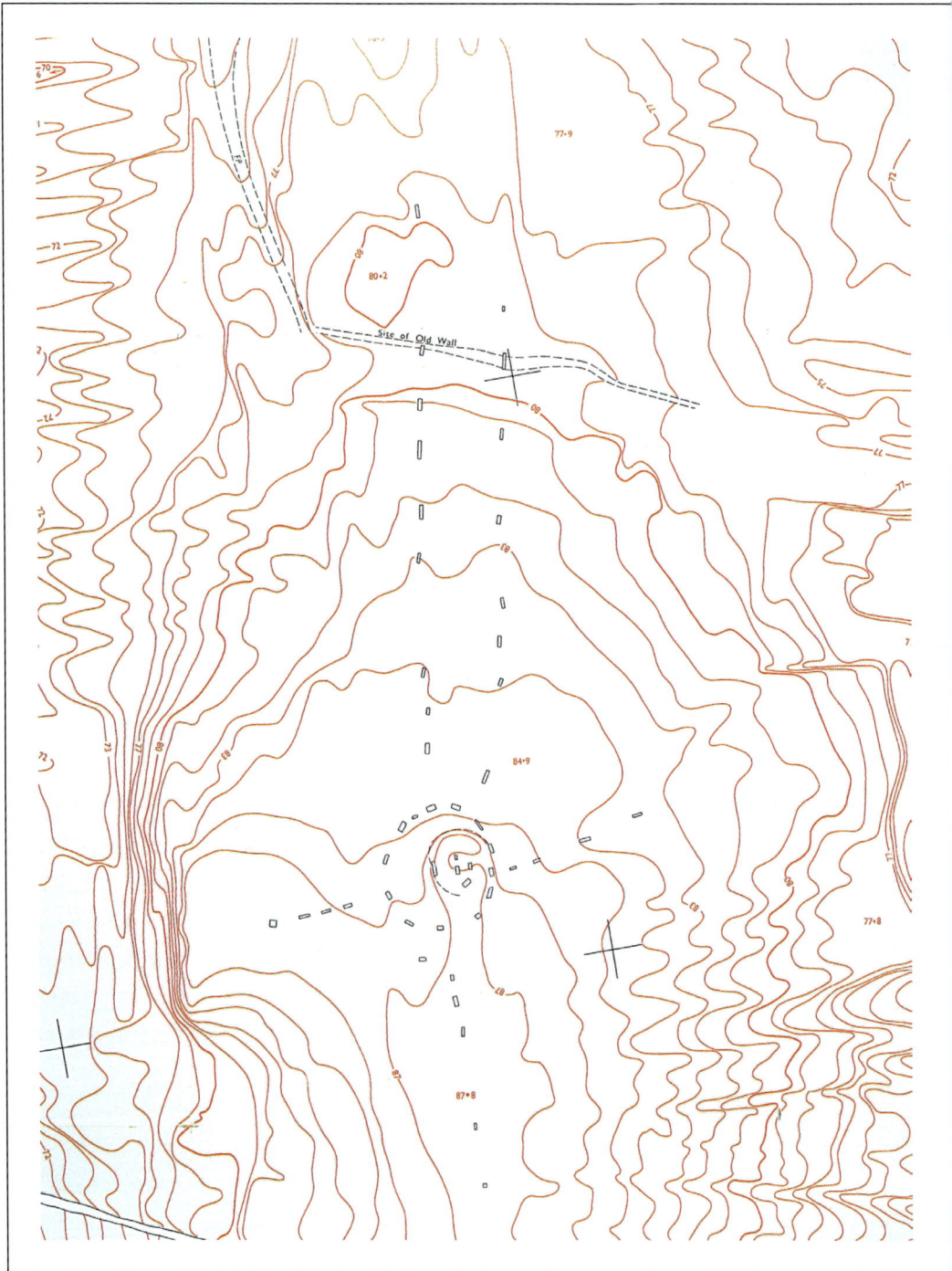

(Left) Gerald Hawkins's photogrammetric plan* of Callanish is very accurate and the only one to show contour lines. They make it clear that the south row, the circle and the avenue are *positioned along the crest of a ridge*. Image - the late Gerald Hawkins.

(Below) The builders may have intended that the stones should be silhouetted against the sky when seen from lower ground to east or west, as in this misty photograph. Applying Occam's Razor, and acting as devil's advocate for my own moon skim theory, do we need a more complex reason why the northern avenue does not lie in a straight line with the south row?

* I contacted the company in Northern Ireland which had performed the original aerial photography. They had not retained the images of Callanish, nor those of six other sites commissioned by Hawkins. These other aerial images had not been submitted to photogrammetry, a loss to research at the time.

generated by computer, are no longer considered valid, but his work was hugely influential.

1965   The journal *Science* published Hawkins' paper *'Callanish, a Scottish Stonehenge'*. Applying computer methods to Somerville's plan, he found twelve alignments between stones that he considered astronomically significant. Most can now be refuted, notably those involving stone 35, as its true prehistoric position is unknown (chapter 11).

1967   In *'Megalithic Sites in Britain'* Alexander Thom erroneously called Callanish a restored site (chapter 9). He introduced a numbering system for the other megalithic sites in the area - II, III, IV, etc.

Thom's all-consuming hobby of surveying stone circles throughout Britain had originally been inspired by a visit to Callanish (chapter 46). His theories created a furore among archaeologists, most of whom could not believe that early peoples had such skills.

- While some 'stone circles' are truly circular, many have slightly non-circular shapes. Thom divided these into categories and described geometrical methods for laying them out.
- Measurements of circles were based on a unit which Thom derived statistically – a unit of 2.72 feet that he named the Megalithic Yard.
- Groupings of stones, often in association with 'notches' in the horizon, frequently indicated astronomical events such as sunrise or set, moonrise or set, at significant dates.

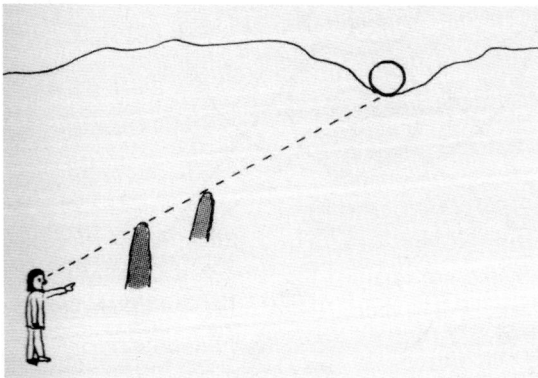

- 'Astronomer-priests' officiating at stone circles were so knowledgeable of the movements of sun and moon that they were capable of predicting eclipses.

1971 National Geographic published Hawkins' paper *A Photogrammetric Survey of Stonehenge and Callanish* (see page 26).

CHAPTER 10

THE LADY AND THE GENERAL

On the Thames embankment, not far from Kew Gardens, stands a large and impressive building. Visiting in the late 1970s, when it was newly opened, we found the strict security and CCTV cameras, so much the norm today, a little oppressive. The foyer is vast and gave us the impression of a hotel, rather than that of a government building, the Public Records Office. Now called the National Archives, it is the government's repository for state documents, ranging from the earliest Parliamentary papers to recent Cabinet minutes.

One might have thought this an unlikely place to find evidence of the past history of Lewis; but follow us on our visit to the PRO, as we search for records of the Standing Stones of Callanish.

Armed only with our new Readers' Tickets and a notebook and pencil each, we are allowed up to the Reading Room, where we are issued with a pager. Fortunately, we already know the general code of the documents we require — WORK 39. From this we find the individual codes of particular documents. We type our details and the codes into a computer terminal (in those days an unfamiliar experience).

We await, over coffee, a signal from the pager to tell us that our documents are ready. The first beep is an electronic error – we are offered

Augustus Lane Fox was a career soldier who rose to the rank of Lieutenant General. In 1880 he inherited a 25,000-acre estate on the borders of Wiltshire and Dorset, obliged under the terms of the will to adopt the surname Pitt Rivers. Investigating sites on his own land in Cranborne Chase, he became Britain's first true archaeologist, with a methodical approach to excavation and recording. His wide-ranging ethnographic interests are still reflected today in the Pitt Rivers Museum in Oxford.

While Pitt Rivers' photographer is unknown, it was Camille Silvy who photographed Lady Mary Jane Matheson in 1862. She became the proprietor of the Isle of Lewis on the death of Sir James in 1878 and retained the island till her death eighteen years later. (Courtesy National Portrait Gallery)

the *Minutes of the Bombing Sub-Committee* for a date in 1942 – and hand them back!

Eventually, we are presented with a small pile of dog-eared notebooks and sketch pads. These are the *actual field notebooks* of General Augustus Pitt Rivers and of his assistant William Tomkin. They had spent two days at the Standing Stones of Callanish, where Tomkin drew each stone and Pitt Rivers recorded the height of each one. This information later proved of great value in our researches on Callanish. Tomkin also painted a water-colour of the stones, probably since lost.

It is clear that they were well-equipped for their trip, with the following items listed – an iron levelling rod, three tapes of 60 or 100 feet, barometer, clinometer, compasses – and for use indoors, a pocket inkstand, pens and a small library of books. Examining the notebooks and a diary, we were interested to learn of their week on Lewis.

They had arrived in Stornoway aboard the *Claymore* at midnight on Saturday 8th August 1885, spending the Sunday on a stroll around the town and onto the quay to see the *'Herring Fishery &c'*. After their time at Callanish, Pitt Rivers and Tomkin drew and measured the Ballantrushal stone and the 'Pictish Tower' of Dun Carloway. They watched an old lady, Flora MacDonald, making craggans from blue clay. From copious records in the notebooks, the beehive sheilings beyond Morsgail Shooting Lodge were given as much attention as the Callanish Stones. On their second Sunday they walked in the Castle Grounds *'with W.N. of Edinboro'*.

An Act for the Protection of Ancient Monuments, influenced by the taking of ancient sites into state care in Denmark, had been passed in 1882. The bill had been introduced by Sir John Lubbock FRS, who was Pitt Rivers' son-in-law, even though the two men were of the same generation. Lubbock was something of a national hero as the MP who had proposed the August Bank Holiday.

The Act listed fifty monuments in Great Britain deserving protection. There was no compulsion to comply, as Victorian landowners strongly resented government interference. Pitt Rivers, in the new post of Chief Inspector of Ancient Monuments, travelled the length and breadth of Great Britain. He was able to persuade many property owners to place their monuments into state Guardianship, perhaps as he was able to talk to landowners on equal terms.

And this is where Lady Mary-Jane Matheson comes into the story. Her husband, Sir James Matheson, had been a partner in the powerful Jardine-Matheson trading company. In 1844 he bought the Isle of Lewis, and had Lews Castle built overlooking Stornoway Harbour. On his death in 1878, Lady Matheson became the owner of the island.

I found useful evidence in an unexpected source – the excellent museum in Salisbury, Wiltshire (not far from the school that I had attended, all those years ago). After Pitt Rivers' death, many of his papers, including much of his correspondence as Inspector, had been deposited in the archives of the nearest major museum to his country estate.

Untying the pink ribbon around a bundle of old papers, I found a most important letter in Lady Matheson's handwriting. She regretted not being in Stornoway at the time of Pitt Rivers' visit but, writing a few months later, she complied with his main request:

> *'I shall be only too glad to have the 'Callernish Stones' and the 'Doune' put under the Ancient Monts. Act and quite believe that it is the only way to preserve them'.*

The letter was headed *'Stornoway N.B.'* (North Britain!), dated Oct. 13th, 1885 and signed, *'Yours very truly, Mary Jane Matheson'.*

Archives can be exciting – I was thrilled to discover and handle that document, ninety years after Lady Matheson had penned it. In the same bundle, I found correspondence between Pitt Rivers, William Mackay (Lady Matheson's factor) and the Office of Works, concerning the protection of Callanish. An iron railing around the site was proposed, but this would have cost £105 and *'the total provision for Ancient Monuments for 1886-7 is only £100'* (the equivalent of £16,600 today). I felt quite glad of that Victorian budget constraint, or in the 1970s Callanish might have been surrounded by rusting iron-work.

Reading M V Thomson's biography of the General, I found a description of the extensive museum collection that Pitt Rivers maintained in his grounds at Tollard Royal in Dorset. One fascinating fact leapt out – *'On the south western part of the site was a Norse Mill brought from the Isle of Lewis'*. In the notebooks we had seen Tomkin's drawing of a Norse Mill at Barvas. Was this the one bought by Augustus Pitt Rivers to transport south and re-erect on his estate in rural Dorset?

CHAPTER 11

DOES CALLANISH LOOK THE SAME AS IN PREHISTORIC TIMES?

There are many stone circles in other parts of Britain.

- Many are just rings of stone.
- Others have a single stone at the centre of the circle.
- Some have an associated burial chamber.
- An extra stone or two may stand just outside the circle.
- There may be a row of stones leading away from the circle.
- Or an avenue leading towards it.

Callanish is unique in possessing *all* of these features.

- A ring of 13 tall megaliths, with a taller one at the centre.
- A chambered cairn fitted within one side of the ring.
- Rows of stones, four to the west, five to the east, five to the south.
- An avenue of 19 stones running roughly northwards.
- Stones that do not fit the overall pattern.

The Callanish circle of thirteen tall megaliths,
with an even taller central stone.

The site's greatest dimension north-south, stone 19 to stone 24, is around 400 feet / 120 meters. East-west, stone 33A to stone 23, the site measures around 150 feet / 46 meters.

Clearly some stone circles were the result of a definite plan. Brodgar in Orkney is believed to have had sixty erect stones, arranged evenly at six degree intervals around the 360° of a perfect circle. Stonehenge was added to and rearranged over the centuries, but the concept of a continuous outer circle of thirty standing stones and thirty lintels, the top *perfectly level* despite a gently sloping site, can only have been conceived by a prehistoric genius – a true architect. But was it ever finished? We cannot be certain.

Was Callanish also a 'grand design'? or did it 'just grow'? was it ever finished? Perhaps more important to us today, are we seeing it just as its users saw it?

35

19

8

Possible 18A

18

**Stones 36-40
are part of the
central cairn**

17

7

16

6

15

5

14

13

4

3

2

1

12

11

10

52 53

51

41

34

50

42

49

29

43,44

23 22 21 20

48

47

45 30 31

32

33

33A

9

46

28

35

27

26

25

24

Once two more
stones in south row ?

Cnoc an Tursa
natural rock
outcrop

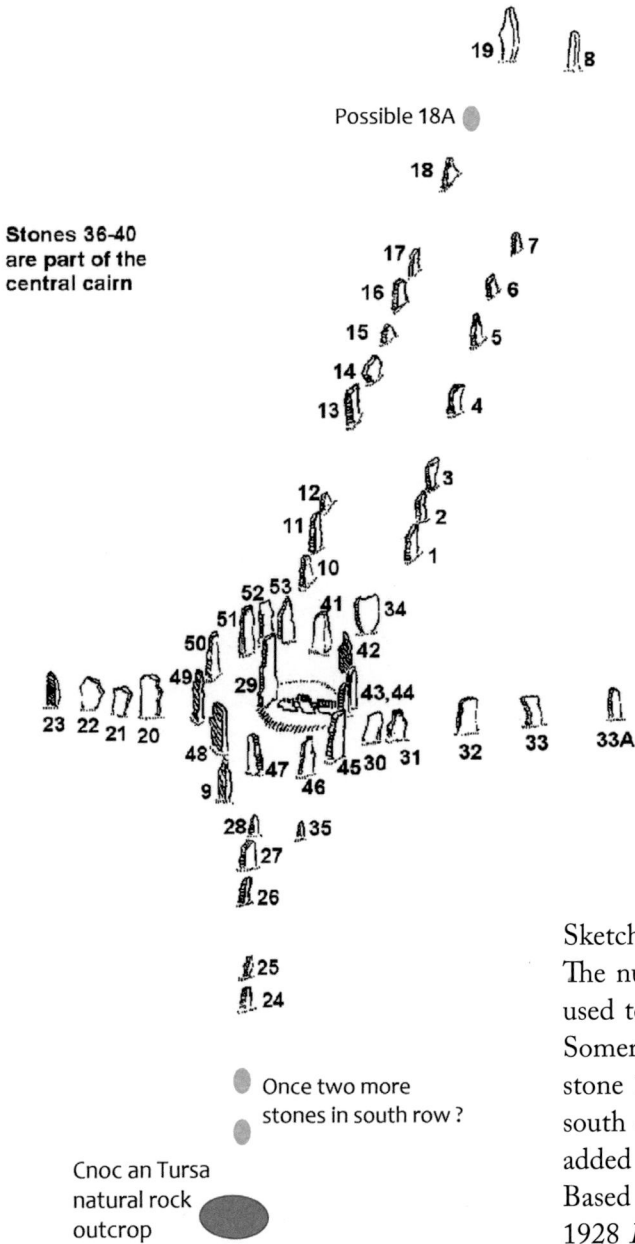

Sketch-plan of Callanish I.
The numbering system still
used today was introduced by
Somerville in 1912. Possible
stone 18A and the features
south of stone 24 have been
added diagrammatically.
Based on a plan in the
1928 *Inventory*.

Before a house was built in an adjoining field, the distant Callanish Stones were visible from our sun-lounge. One morning, casually looking in that direction, I noticed the jib of a crane. Checking through binoculars it appeared to be very near the Stones. I grabbed my camera bag and drove to the site. Sure enough, a mobile crane was parked there, with a photographer suspended in a personnel basket over the avenue. When he was back on the ground, he told me that he was taking aerial shots for the Ancient Monuments department, having hired the crane as there was no pilot available with a light plane. Explaining my interest, I asked if I might take some shots. So, with no Health and Safety regulations in the 1970s, I had another mini-adventure, lifted into a position where I could take this photograph.

The layout of the site is very clear. In the foreground, the avenue leads up to the circle with the east row off to the left and two stones of the west row off to the right. Beyond the circle is the south row, and on the other side of the wall, the rocky outcrop of Cnoc an Tursa.

Was the Site Restored ?

In the late 1970s, Margaret and I pored over many maps, plans and drawings, investigating the idea that Callanish had been 'restored' in the 19th century.

In *'Megalithic Sites in Britain'*, Professor Alexander Thom had written that John MacCulloch's 1819 plan *'seems to be the only record, albeit difficult to interpret, of the stones which were upright before the reconstruction which took place later'* while in another book he wrote *'fallen stones were subsequently re-erected'*.

Interpreting MacCulloch's plan required our access to sources not seen by Thom.

- From Nationalmuseet, Copenhagen, we obtained copies of field notebooks recording Jacob Worsaae's visit to Callanish in 1846.
- We purchased a photocopy from an Edinburgh library of an 1854 engraving by Henry Kerr.
- From Southampton, we borrowed a huge book with an 1867 drawing by Sir Henry James, director of the Ordnance Survey.
- As already explained, we had obtained copies of William Tomkin's 1885 field sketches of each stone.

In 1857, at the direction of Sir James Matheson, peat was cleared from around the stones of the circle, revealing the chambered cairn at the centre. From evidence available, it seems likely that this was a single day's work, no doubt carried out by a large team of estate workers, on October 2nd.

Worsaae and Kerr had visited before this; James and Tomkin came after this clearance. Taking the four sources together, it became very clear that the stones had been deeply embedded in peat prior to 1857.

MacCulloch had walked on a *land surface five feet higher than today's*. When he recorded ten stones in the avenue as fallen, what he actually saw were the exposed tops of much larger stones, mostly buried in the peat. Thus Thom's assumption of a restoration, based on these supposedly fallen stones, was incorrect.

When Jacob Worsaae visited the Hebrides from Denmark in 1846, his interest was mainly in the Viking era. But he visited Callanish and made two sketches in his field notebook. As the earliest known drawings of the site they provide valuable evidence. The upper illustration shows the circle stones much shorter than they appear today, eleven years before the peat was removed from around their bases. The lower sketch reveals that peat had already been taken from the avenue for use as household fuel. Image © Nationalmuseet, Copenhagen.

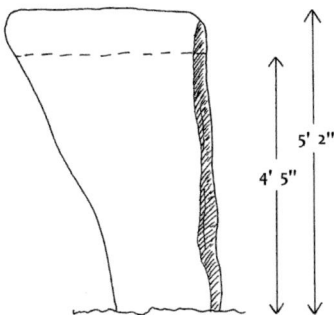

When General Pitt Rivers visited Callanish, his assistant drew individual stones. In each case, as in this drawing of stone 3, he indicated the 'tide mark' still visible 28 years after the clearance of peat. Visitors before 1857 would have seen only that part of the stone above the dotted line. Redrawn from William Tomkin, 1885.

39

This is a hugely important image for our understanding of Callanish.
Nearly ten years after the enveloping peat was removed, the bleached
lower part of each stone reveals the former ground level.

A drawing by Sir Henry James, Director General of the Ordnance Survey,
was 'copied in chalk' by Second Corporal Goodwin RE and published
in James's book *'Stonehenge and Turusachan on the Island of Lewis'*
(1867, Ordnance Survey).

Nineteen, or More, Stones in the Avenue

Martin Martin had published a plan of Callanish in 1700 showing
nineteen stones *on each side* of the northern avenue, when today the total
on both sides is nineteen. Despite other inaccuracies in the plan, some
writers believed him. We consider it a major error, perhaps, as William
Borlase suggested, by *'some inaccurate engraver'*.

We rejected suggestions that the avenue was once longer, with more stones north of stones 8 and 19. Their shapes are such that they may be considered 'blocking stones', a feature known to mark the ends of other megalithic stone rows.

If any stones had been damaged in Viking or medieval times, with peat already protecting their lower sections, they would have been truncated at two to four feet high, with broken-off tips left lying within the peat.

MacCulloch's plan of the west side of the avenue included five more stones than are present today, so we wondered if any really had been lost since 1819. The protective peat began to be cleared as Callanish villagers sourced fuel, probably from around 1825. At that date, as part of the notorious Highland Clearances, crofters evicted from the relatively fertile land at Linshader were resettled at Callanish.

We know from Worsaae's sketches that much of the avenue had been cleared of peat, almost to the circle, by 1846. If an avenue stone fell as peat was cleared, it would have been considered useful construction material for village houses. Packing stones might remain as evidence in the soil today.

A Physical Search for Possible Lost Stones

Anyone who has watched 'Time Team' will know about geophysics – the use of electronic gear to explore below ground level without excavation. At the start of August 1979, Patrick Ashmore used early and basic soil resistivity equipment across the whole of the Callanish site.

Mary Harman, 'Mary Bones', a freelance bone expert, stayed with us for a week, while our children were on their own separate holidays. Working together on site, Mary laid out tape grids, I operated the pair of unwieldy probes, inserting them into the turf at regular intervals, Patrick took readings from a meter, while Margaret recorded them on a clipboard. A single operator and modern equipment could do the task in a matter of hours, producing an electronic chart. The onsite work took the four of us several days and the chart then had to be plotted on paper by hand.

During his 1980 excavation, Patrick Ashmore chose the position of some trenches on the basis of the resistivity results. In a trench between stones 18 and 19, the team found a definite socket for a former standing stone (which we might call 18A). A nearby feature may have been a second socket. Other 'structures' revealed by the resistivity results proved to be bedrock, just below the turf.

The South Row and Cnoc an Tursa

In 1984, we wrote that *'the circle of 13 stones is almost certainly intact and the west and south rows may well be complete as they stand today'*. (See chapter 13 concerning the stones of the east row.) There have since been new discoveries concerning the south row and the natural rock formation of Cnoc an Tursa (hillock of sadness). Excavated socket holes suggest that there may once have been two more stones between stone 24, at present the most southerly of the south row, and Cnoc an Tursa. They are tentatively shown on my plan.

A slit in Cnoc an Tursa is aligned north-south, so that the midday sun creates a beam of light towards the south row, first noticed in modern times by Ian McHardy in 1993. Due to the varying height of the sun in the sky, the beam is much longer in the winter than in the summer.

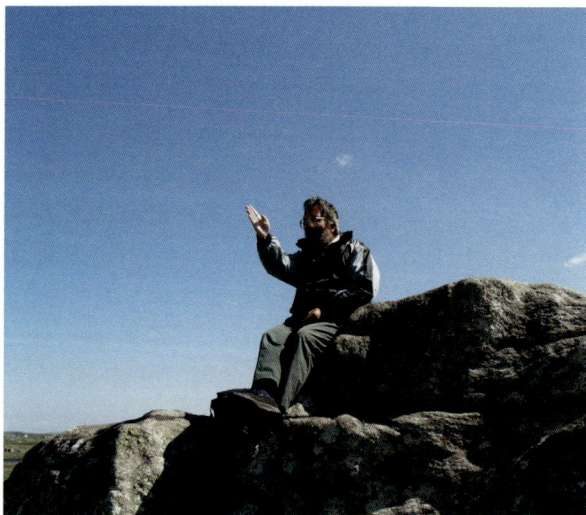

On the upper northern side of Cnoc an Tursa there is a natural 'rock seat' which proves surprisingly comfortable. Sitting there, I am looking due north along the south row towards the central megalith. The slit which creates a midday sunbeam is just below my feet.

This must have been noticed in ancient times and may have been used as a simple calendar.

Excavations in front of and on the top of Cnoc an Tursa revealed ancient activity in both areas. It is possible that Cnoc an Tursa had been a revered site before the first megaliths were erected.

The 'Extra' Stones

If we consider the Callanish layout as a circle, a central stone and five stone rows, then stones 9, 35 and 34 can be considered 'extraneous' stones. Stone 34 is perhaps part of the avenue, but it is out of alignment with the rest of the stones in the eastern arm.

Stone 9 stands to the southwest of the circle. There is no indication that it once formed part of an outer circle, as theorised by Aubrey Burl. Somerville's moon alignment from stone 9 to stone 34 remains the only theory that attempts to justify its position. The next section is devoted to stone 35.

We found no documentary evidence for suggestions that the south, east or west rows once had partners, making them into avenues, nor was any physical evidence found in the excavations.

Broken, Repaired, Re-Erected

Stone 35 is the smallest stone at the site and has the most chequered history. It was missing from all early plans, being first mentioned by Henry Sharbau in 1860, the only stone recorded by him as 'fallen'. It seems likely that it fell in antiquity and had lain beneath the peat for millennia.

By the time of James's plan of 1867 it had been erected symmetrically across from stone 28, a stone of similar size. Walking from the gate towards the circle along 'Lady Matheson's Path', the pair formed a sort of 'entranceway', which would have appealed to Victorian sensibilities. We assumed that 35 was erected at the same time that the path was laid for the convenience of visitors from Lews Castle.

In a picture postcard from around 1878, stone 35 is shown broken, the lower half remaining erect. We were told of a local tradition - the stone was broken, generations back, by a drunk while waiting for the ferry from Callanish Pier to Great Bernera, and that he was imprisoned for this offence.

Retuning to the bundle of letters that I found in Salisbury, Pitt Rivers wrote to factor William MacKay on September 14th 1885, thanking him for his help at Callanish, and continued:

'The stone I spoke to you about ought certainly to be cemented in before it gets lost. The broken half now lies at the foot of its standing stump. With the help of two others I put it up to see if it fitted accurately and found that it did so, but it was not safe to leave it on and so I replaced it at the foot of the stump.'

Clearly MacKay did not take action on this, as the stone still appears in its broken state in an engraving dated 1891 and in a number of

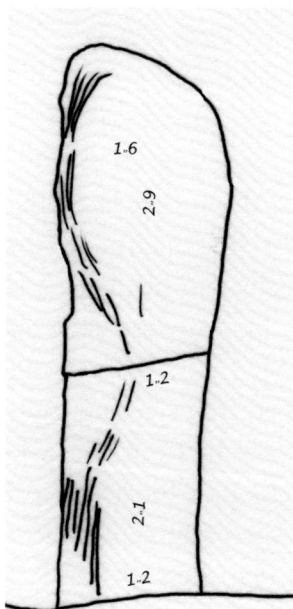

When we examined Pitt Rivers' notebooks on our visit to the PRO at Kew, we were excited to find that the General had drawn stone 35 himself, rather than leaving it to his assistant. The sketch shows the breakage and is annotated *'Stone lying outside of circle S4°W of centre. Stone pulled up by us & 18 feet outside circle'*. Redrawn, with measurements in feet and inches clarified, from Pitt Rivers, 1885.

photographs taken around the turn of the twentieth century. However, it had been repaired before Somerville's plan of 1912.

During the 1981 excavations, a trench was opened around stone 35, soon showing that its base was set in concrete. Once the stone was lifted and the concrete chipped away, attempts were made to find its true prehistoric socket hole. A hole was found – but it was not a fit for either end of stone 35.

So stone 35 was re-erected in the same spot that had been chosen in Victorian times. Its original prehistoric position remains unknown, so any theories based on the position of this stone must be discarded.

The Burial Chamber

From the excavation, we know that the chambered cairn is later than the circle and that it went through different phases in prehistory.

This 'wide angle sketch' does not give a very good impression of the burial chamber. However, I am including it here as it is one of only two drawings known before the earliest photograph of 1923. Henry Sharbau's sketch has been reprinted in a number of books, but Christine Maclagan's has remained in the archives, apart from its appearance in my *Gazette* column of September 30th 1983.

She once made the acerbic remark that, as a woman, she was considered '*unworthy of being a member of any antiquarian society*'. Redrawn from Maclagan, 1879 .

'Improvements' were made in Victorian times. Some careful restoration was undertaken during the 1981 dig, since when there has been unfortunate deterioration due to the number of visitors. None of this alters the appearance of the site as a whole.

Were Stone Circles Ever 'Finished'?

Some archaeologists believe that, for the builders of stone circles, the process of finding, transporting and erecting the megaliths was of greater importance to the community than the finished project. And did these early societies actually have a concept of a structure being completed?

The Callanish circle, with its tall central stone, was probably constructed as a single project, though some think that stone 52 was an afterthought, 'squeezed into the gap' between 51 and 53.

The stone rows and the chambered cairn probably came up to 500 years later. The east and west rows are almost certainly complete. The south row has probably lost two stones. The 'gaps' in each side of the avenue may be due to lost stones; or may be due to stones being added gradually over the years; or there may have been gaps for reasons that cannot be known to us.

Today, the avenue still slopes invitingly upwards along the ridge to the circle. As we stand within the tall enclosing stones and look along the radiating rows to the subtle browns and greens and greys of the moors and hills, we can imagine our prehistoric forebears doing the same. We feel confident that, thanks to centuries of enveloping peat, they knew the Callanish Stones much as we see them today.

CHAPTER 12

'*THE STANDING STONES OF CALLANISH*'

Late in the afternoon of May 26th 1977, I was standing on a pavement in Stornoway, feeling extremely pleased with myself. In my hand, I held a proper printed copy of a book that I had written and published – and there was a display of copies in the bookshop window.

A few months earlier, and less than two years since we had started serious studies of the Callanish Stones, I felt that I had gathered enough information to write the first-ever tourist guide. At that point, the only information about Callanish for visitors was provided by an on-site metal notice and a four-page leaflet on sale for 1p at Arnol Black House! Neither was particularly informative.

So I wrote a draft text and printed black-and-white photos to illustrate it. Initially this was my project, but when Margaret decided to 'come on board' she suggested improvements to my text, which was also checked by interested friends. She drew plans and diagrams to supplement my photos, including an annotated double-page site plan. We pasted copies of our material, page by page, into a scrapbook as a possible guide for a printer.

We approached the Highlands and Islands Development Board and at least six other local and national organisations, hoping for publication or sponsorship … all in vain. Could we do it ourselves? Self-publication was not common in those days.

We went to see Chris Weir, proprietor of small Stornoway company, Essprint. He perused our scrapbook and examined the original material. He quoted a printing cost of £445, a very big sum for a family living on a teacher's salary. (The equivalent in 2025 would be around £3540.)

Then Chris said something I have never forgotten – and have always remained grateful for. *I'm sure you have a best seller here. I will not ask for payment for the first thousand copies till you come back and order a second thousand.'* Talk about an offer we could not refuse! We ordered the print run.

Creating a book was much more complicated in those pre-computer days. Every word had to be retyped by Essprint staff. Each illustration had to be photographed on a room-sized camera, before page layouts were designed and prepared for the press. Over a few weeks, I called at Essprint from time to time to check on progress, while also approaching possible sales outlets.

Essprint of course were just the printers; we became publishers, registering the imprint 'G & M Ponting' and acquiring our first ISBN (International Standard Book Number 0950599808).

In a major advertising scoop, I persuaded MacIver and Dart to let me take over their regular spot on the front page of the *Stornoway Gazette*. As well as televisions and radios, their shop stocked photographic materials. The week that our little 32-page book appeared, priced at 75 pence, my advert described its contents and ended ... *All photographs in the book were taken on Ilford film and printed on Kodak paper purchased from MACIVER AND DART'*.

Roddy Smith's newsagents and stationers, a thriving business in a prominent position in Stornoway town centre, took 300 copies on the first day. I took boxes of books home, but it was not long before Smith's and other outlets reordered. We sold many individual copies by post. Edwin Krupp* ordered fifty copies to be posted to Los Angeles!

Favourable reviews of our book appeared in the press across Scotland. It was soon clear that Chris had been correct when he predicted a best seller. I ordered a second printing as early as July and it sold an incredible 2500 copies in the first year – an exciting period! Our bank manager suggested that we should open a Callanish Stones Account, separate

---

* In 2025, Edwin Krupp is still in post as director of Los Angeles' Griffith Observatory, maintaining his considerable interest in connections between ancient sites and the heavens.

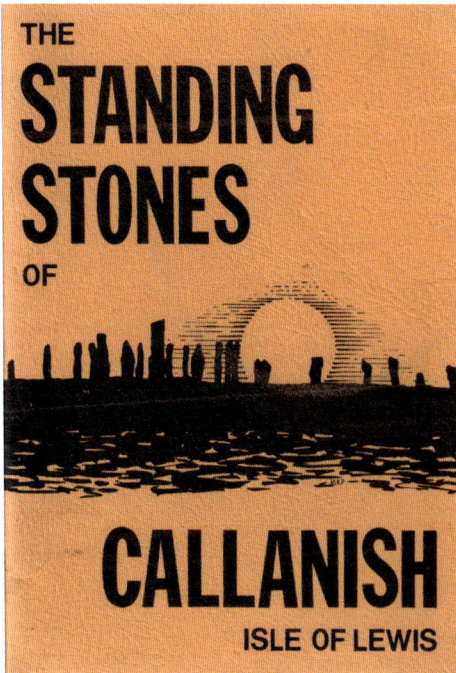

Our first publication. The silhouette which we designed for the book cover became our logo, which in due course we also used on a range of T-shirts. Sales of books and T-shirts financed our continuing research.

from any personal account. We found ourselves, in effect, running a small business, the 'Callanish Megalithic Research Project'.

Over a seven-year period, total sales of our self-published guidebook totalled 13,000 copies. Since my return to Hampshire I have self-published other books, mostly on local history. Receiving the first copy has always been exciting, but has never quite equalled the thrill on that day in May 1977.

Surprisingly, our little book, 40 years out of print, may now be perused in full online thanks to the Internet Archive website.

CHAPTER 13

A STONE RESTORED
TO THE EAST ROW

Our study of an old plan by Lieutenant John Lynton Palmer led us to a major discovery and eventually to the re-erection of a lost stone at the site.

Palmer's plan, labelled *'Stones of Callernish Lewis Hebrides'*, dates from 1857 and was probably prepared not long before peat was cleared from the circle. It survives in an Edinburgh archive only as a copy on a large sheet of tracing paper, but it is useful, as he recorded the measurements in feet and inches between each stone and the next.

Finding the Stone, February 17th-18th 1979

One-hundred-and-forty years later, we checked his accuracy, spending two days with pegs, metre tapes and clipboard to take our own measurements. On the whole we found his figures reliable - but there was a major anomaly. He showed six stones in the East Row instead of four.

One of the extras was without doubt an error. The distance between stone 44 (east side of the circle) and stone 30 (in the east row, nearest the circle) is eight feet. The figure '8' that must have been on Palmer's original plan was wrongly traced as an extra stone.

However, the apparent stone nineteen feet beyond stone 33, at the east end of the east row, could not be explained away so readily. We gave it the code name 33A. Examining the very corner of James Kerr's 1854 engraving, part of a stone can be seen. It is in the right position to be another possible record of 33A, three years before Palmer's visit.

As 33A's location was outside the site fence, we did not need official permission to investigate. It was on the croft land of Angus Morrison, our postman, and he was very happy for us to 'poke around'. With modern technology and with a suitable budget the stone could have been found electronically in moments. But our basic 'geophysics device', specially created for us by the Stornoway blacksmith, was a blunt-ended iron rod, graduated in centimetres, and with a wooden handle (seen in a photograph in chapter 22). An initial 'poke' immediately confirmed that there was 'something rocky' beneath the turf.

To investigate, we laid out a grid with string and pegs, eight-metres on each side. Over two days, we probed systematically at regular intervals across the grid. At each point, we recorded the depth to which the probe could be pushed. This proved to be 40 - 70 cm over most of the area, but only 5 - 25 cm when the probe contacted rock. Using this data, we established the size and approximate shape of the buried megalith.

We pegged white slips of paper to indicate an outline of the stone … and my photograph of this was later published in *'Current Archaeology'* magazine. When we showed Angus, he offered to dash off for a spade … but we took a responsible approach, so had to wait before 33A could be exposed. We sent all our data to Patrick Ashmore at the Ancient Monuments department in Edinburgh

Uncovering the Stone, May 1st 1980

When Patrick started his major excavation at Callanish, one of the first trenches to be opened was intended to expose 33A. Margaret and other volunteer diggers spent a day stripping turf and opening up a trench on our predicted spot.

However, it was a teaching day for me, so when I returned from Stornoway on the school bus, I immediately walked up to the site, uncertain of what I would find. There was Stone 33A uncovered, lying in the trench – yes! Patrick was already talking about the possibility of re-erecting it.

Stone 33A revealed at last, over two years after we had proved its existence beneath the turf, a wonderful justification for our studies. It was a great thrill to see it exposed by the excavation team.

Lifting the Stone, May 14th 1981

I must somehow have wangled a way to skip my morning's teaching duties, as I was on site in bright sunshine by 8:30 a.m., watching the Ancient Monuments work-force set up a scaffolding tripod over the stone, ready for the lift.

The event developed an almost carnival atmosphere. The older pupils from Breasclete Primary, instead of going directly to school, gathered at the stones. A small school, its pupils between the ages of 5 and 12 occupied three rooms, each with one teacher. While preparatory work was being carried out, I took the pupils from the 'top two rooms' on a guided tour of the site … a site which they must have known all their lives.

Margaret and two other helpers knelt in the trench and cleared enough soil from under the stone to fit nylon straps around it. By now all of the excavation team had arrived, soon joined by the group of artists who were camped nearby (chapter 18). Also, the children from the 'lower room' were brought from the school by their teacher. There must have been up to a hundred people present, including local stringer, Bill Lucas, taking stills and cine film for local and national media.

Workmen used the straps under the stone as a sling and connected it to a block-and-tackle pulley system. One man balanced precariously on the tripod frame and started slowly operating a lever. The stone shifted slightly and we all held our breath in case it should slip or break. Soon, it was dangling over the trench. Still suspended, it was man-handled to one side and laid down on the grass.

As the tripod was disassembled and the children trooped the mile or so back to the school, Bill Lucas interviewed Patrick, then offered me a lift to Stornoway, where he interviewed me in the car. I was back in my biology class by 11:30 after a memorable morning.

The following day our two interviews were slotted together on Inverness-based BBC Radio Highland and on Stornoway's Radio nan Eilean. Bill's photographs appeared, not just in the *Stornoway Gazette*, but also in the Aberdeen *Press and Journal*, *The Scotsman* and *The Times*. I had notified Bill of the coming event without reference to Patrick – who, at first, was not best pleased by the unwanted publicity!

Waiting for the Lawyers, 1981-2

Excavation in the trench soon revealed a socket hole with packing stones, strongly suggesting that the stone had once been erect. But it could not be restored immediately, as it was not within the site fence. It was cocooned in plastic, covered with a pile of turf, and left there for over a year.

A small part of Angus's croft, where the stone once stood, needed to be enclosed within the site, while a compensatory area of land had to be transferred from the site to the croft. With both croftland and Ancient

Monuments land protected, if not inalienable, it took Edinburgh lawyers some months to negotiate the exchange. Once sorted, the fence was moved to the new line.

Re-Erecting the Stone, July 20th 1982

At the time that 33A was being re-erected, I was crossing from Ullapool to Stornoway, my return from the south of England delayed by rail strikes. In fact, I had been given a lift as far as Fort William by a kind motorist who had responded to my appeal on a Bournemouth radio station! In due course I was able to see the event on television, as it had been filmed by the BBC and was shown as a segment in Magnus Magnusson's one-off documentary *'Echoes in Stone'*.

Using similar equipment to that for the initial lifting, the stone was raised to a vertical position. Then, gently, so gently, it was lowered towards its socket hole. Patrick was on his knees, steering it to the correct orientation.

When I arrived on site later that day, it was a thrill to see 33A erect at last, five years and five months since we had proved its existence. It was still supported by scaffolding and I watched as several wheelbarrow-loads of concrete were poured in. A few packing stones around the base had proved sufficient for the prehistoric builders!

Revisiting the Stone, May 28th 1998

Back on Lewis as a holidaymaker after many years away, I felt greatly pleased to see the Callanish east row complete with its fifth stone. Now recorded officially as 'Stone 33A' in the new Visitor Centre, it had been such a central part of my life for several years.

CHAPTER 14

THE STORY OF STONE 19

Stone 19 is the distinctive tall stone that is the most northerly on the west side of the Callanish Avenue. Thanks to our documentary researches, it regained several inches in height in 1978.

We had found early records of each stone. In 1860, Henry Sharbau, assistant to Captain F W L Thomas, made delicate pencil sketches of every megalith at the site, recording the height of each one. The field notebooks of General Pitt Rivers and his assistant William Tomkin, already mentioned, included drawings and measurements of each stone. The RCAHMS Inventory included height measurements taken in 1914.

Tabulating these three sets of figures from 1860, 1885 and 1914, we found a number of significant disagreements. When a later measurement was shorter than an earlier one, was this because the stone had actually been damaged in the intervening years? We decided to investigate by taking our own measurements and visually checking the top of each stone.

In February 1978 we arrived at the site in brilliant sunshine, but our work was later interrupted by a brief heavy snow shower, creating mini-drifts in crevices in the megaliths. At each stone, we placed a wooden bar horizontally across the tip and measured down to ground level, often taking slightly different values on opposite sides, where the ground sloped. For the loftier stones, I stood on a tall step-ladder loaned by Breasclete School, held the bar in place and dropped the metric tape for Margaret to record the reading. We later converted our metric measurements to feet and inches for direct comparison with the earlier values.

We also noted any obvious damage to the stones, finding that 32 of the 48 showed some form of minor damage. This included those where brownish or greyish-white 'cement' had at some point in the past been used to fill cracks. Stone 49 on the east side of the circle formerly had a projection on its north side, two or three feet from ground level – it appears in Sharbau's drawing and on a postcard of about 1878, but not in Tomkin's drawing (1885), so that it must have been damaged in the few years between those dates.

Our recorded heights of eleven stones differed significantly from at least two of the three previous records. This could often be explained by differences in ground level, varying methods of measurement, even the growth of vegetation – our work in February must have been easier than Pitt Rivers' in August.

However, for three stones, 12, 19 and 23, the discrepancy was explained by the clearly damaged upper surface. Stone 12 (east side of avenue) is around 30 cm shorter than when it was drawn by Sharbau with a

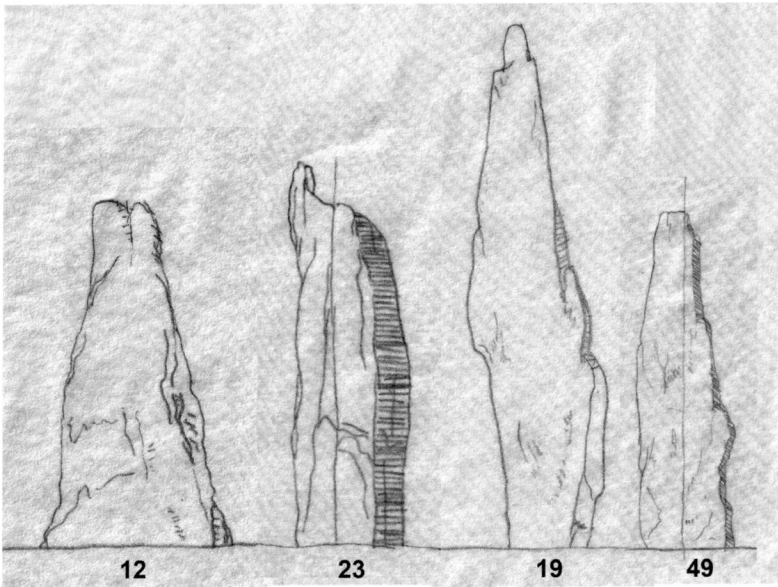

A compilation of four pencil drawings of individual stones by Henry Sharbau, seen undamaged in 1860. Later, stones 12, 23 and 19 suffered damage to their tops, while stone 49 lost a projection on its side. Redrawn in 2002 by K. L'Estrange for 'Callanish'.

bifurcated tip; it was broken once before 1885 and again later. Stone 23 (end of west row) lost a knob on its upper surface between 1860 and 1885. We thought that up to another fourteen stones had smaller pieces missing from their top surface.

However, it is the story of Stone 19 that always intrigues visitors, whether tourists or experts. The loss of about 20 cm between the visits of Sharbau and Tomkin is very clear from their drawings. When taking our measurements, we had worked from the south of the site to the north, so that stone 19 happened to be the last one for us to measure.

As it is one of the tallest stones, I climbed the step-ladder and found that the upper surface had sharply-angled edges, consistent with the known break. Margaret recorded the measurements and I started to collapse the ladder, ready to head homewards.

Then came the greatest moment of serendipity in the whole of our studies. Margaret said – *'I think I have found the broken tip'* – I was inevitably incredulous. But she had found a rock, roughly football-sized, within the low stone wall that formed the northern boundary of the site.

I set up the ladder again and she handed me the rock. Now starting to believe that this was possible, I carried the rock as I climbed. After working out the orientation, I found that Margaret's rock *was a perfect*

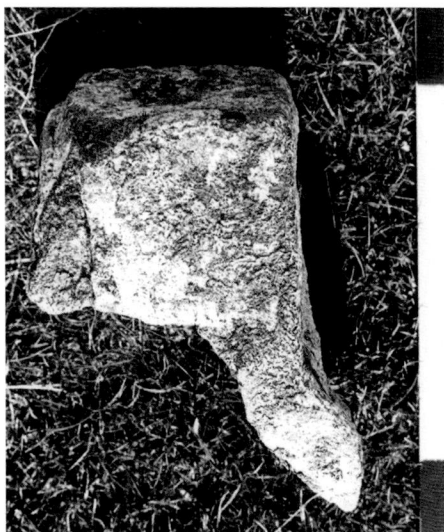

Beside a 10cm scale, the tip of stone 19 does not look particularly big, but was a sizeable chunk of rock!

(Left) The moment when I found that the rock discovered by Margaret was a good fit to the damaged top of stone 19.

(Right) Neil Macphee in the process of gluing the tip of stone 19 in place.

fit for the broken top. It had lain nearby, unnoticed, for around one hundred years. This was one of the most exciting moments in our 'archaeological adventures'!

We took the broken-off piece home and notified the appropriate authorities. It proved a fascinating item to show visitors who came to talk to us about Callanish.

After six months, Neil MacPhee of the Ancient Monuments workforce took the rock, climbed a ladder and glued the broken piece back in place. A photograph of this restoration appeared on the front page of the *Stornoway Gazette* under the headline *'TIP FOR THE TOP'*.

CHAPTER 15

DIARY OF AN
ARCHAEOLOGICAL AWARD

As recorded in my personal diary, with details from an article in *Current Archaeology*.

Monday December 19th 1977

As regular viewers of the BBC archaeology series *'Chronicle'*, we watched an 'awards for amateurs' episode. Six short films featured groups which had made it to the finals, with a presentation to the winner. We immediately decided to enter the following year.

Thursday February 23rd 1978

We received entry requirements - submit a 1000-word summary of our researches, supported by up to six illustrations.

Thursday March 16th

We posted our concise account and charts. We included our documentary studies, our finds of additional sites, our discovery of stone 33A (still below the turf), our publication of the first guidebook and our recent finding of the tip of stone 19.

Tuesday May 2nd

We were excited to be invited, as finalists, to give a 17-minute presentation in London – in under two weeks' time! As well as choosing slides for our presentation, we had to plan our travel and to make arrangements for children and animals during our absence.

Saturday May 13th

We had flown from Stornoway on Friday, then taken the sleeper train from Inverness to Euston. At a buffet lunch in the Museum of London, we met the judges and the other finalists, as well as staff from the award sponsors – BBC *Chronicle* and Rescue, the British Archaeological Trust. The presentations took place in the Museum lecture theatre in the afternoon, chaired by Magnus Magnusson.

We waited our turn while the other finalists gave their talks on aerial archaeology; cider making equipment; historic buildings in Dunstable; Roman potteries in Alice Holt Forest; and surveys of a military training area in Northumberland. We sat there, palms sweating, till finally it was our turn.

Nerves abated once we took the podium and we felt that we made a real connection with the one hundred or so archaeologists in the audience from our opening remarks.

'If the Standing Stones of Callanish were situated on English downland, rather than on remote Hebridean moorland, they would be one of Britain's major tourist attractions, and would have commanded a research effort comparable to that devoted to Stonehenge. As it is, the stones enjoy a quality of remoteness which is appreciated by many visitors – and research has been a small and piecemeal effort by experts who have each spent a week or two on the island. We thus have an advantage given to few amateurs, a megalithic monument of major importance, only a mile from our home, which has never before had a long-term, in-depth research effort devoted to it.'

Sunday May 14th

Before catching the sleeper train back to Inverness, we visited the Dominion cinema to see *'Star Wars'*, the original film, just a few months after its first release. We were 'blown away' by surround sound and the effects on the huge screen, perhaps specially impressed as there was then no cinema in Stornoway!

Saturday July 8th – Wednesday 12th

A BBC crew spent four days on Lewis filming our work in order to produce a six-minute segment for *Chronicle* – producers Ken and Jill, cameramen Mark and Mick, and sound recordist Louis. As we could not be seen 'working' on Sunday, they shot documentary material indoors. One of the team considered that Lewis Sabbath restrictions were *a barbaric custom unmatched in my extensive travels'* (not my words!). Monday and Tuesday were sunny and warm, perfect for the on-site filming. We re-enacted probing for 33A and I climbed a ladder with the detached tip of Stone 19.

With crews booked to film other finalists in England, Ken and his friends felt that they had 'hit the jackpot' with a working trip to the Hebrides. We shared picnics on leisure visits to beaches, so that it proved a very enjoyable few days.

Wednesday August 9th – Thursday 10th

Time to impress two of the judges in person! Richard Kiln, secretary of Rescue, made his Lewis visit a short family holiday, but Andrew Saunders, Inspector of Ancient Monuments for England, flew up specifically to meet us. We explained our paperwork in the house; Andrew's job title made him a direct successor to Pitt Rivers and we were delighted to show him some of the General's work from 1885. We gave them a tour of the Callanish Stones and visited several of the sites that we had discovered.

The next day, we took them to other sites, unconnected with the judging. At Arnol Black House, a scheduled Ancient Monument, Andrew showed his free staff pass. The elderly lady selling tickets did not recognise it and asked the incognito Inspector of Ancient Monuments if it was up to date!

Tuesday November 7th

After a family morning in London, our children and their grandparents spent the afternoon at the Tower of London, while Margaret and I headed for the British Museum. With other finalists we were invited to a buffet lunch in the Director's House, before the Awards ceremony began in the Lecture Theatre. The awards in categories for Young Archaeologists, for Professionals and for Businesses were presented first.

The Amateur awards were introduced by screening the *Chronicle* film, including our segment. Professor Colin Renfrew, chief of the judging panel, was very complimentary in his summary of our work. However, the *Chronicle* award was presented to the Alice Holt Study Group.

But there was also a 'Legal and General Award for Initiative', open to entrants in all categories, not just to the amateurs. It was won by an English Heritage project at Dover Castle … and we were announced as runners-up. We stepped up to the podium to shake hands with the archaeology graduate handing out the awards – Charles, Prince of Wales (as he then was). He presented us with a £100 cheque and we later received a case of champagne.

Presentations over, everyone moved into the museum galleries, where finalists were invited to have tea with the Prince. We had a memorable conversation with him, overshadowed by the huge Assyrian sculpture of a winged bull. This was followed by a drinks party in the Director's House, where we were interviewed for Radio 4 'Origins'. Later in the day, we headed north again on the Inverness sleeper.

December

The monthly issue of *Current Archaeology* appeared, almost all of it devoted to the work of the six amateur finalists. Four pages on our work at Callanish included seven of our illustrations.

Receiving our presentation from Prince Charles, with Professor Colin Renfrew, chief judge, looking on. Image © British Museum

Monday December 18th

The episode of *Chronicle* including our segment was shown on BBC1. We were pleased that it included Colin Renfrew's comments, but disappointed that it did not mention our Legal and General award. In the days before video recorders were a household item, a timed recording had been set in the science department of the Nicolson Institute – I still have a copy.

We felt that the award, the magazine article and the TV spot provided a very satisfying validation of our studies so far – with two all-expenses-paid visits to London thrown in! A spin-off was that, when Magnus

In a scene from the *Chronicle* episode featuring the finalists, we were comparing an old engraving with the Stones as they appear today.

Magnusson later paid a private visit to Lewis, we gave him a full tour of the Callanish sites. In 1984, he provided a generous foreword for our book, '*New Light on the Stones of Callanish*'.

CHAPTER 16

MORE STONES AROUND CALLANISH

There are three other stone circles within three kilometres of the main Callanish site, each of which would have a much greater reputation were it not overshadowed by its illustrious neighbour. There are other single megaliths and groups of stones in the surrounding countryside. In 1984 I compiled a field guide with details of all these sites – '*The Stones Around Callanish*'.

The three circles had peat cleared from around the bases of the stones in 1858, and had been recognised by some early writers. At the time of my book none of the sites had been the subject of archaeological studies.

Professor Thom had designated the known sites as Callanish I, II, III, IV, V, VI and VII. A team of student surveyors from Glasgow University

Geography Department, led by David Tait, prepared an excellent and useful map of the Callanish area, marking the position of each site. They found other locations and extended the numbering … VIII, IX, X, XI and XII.

As we found more sites, we extended the numbering further, up to XIX – and recorded each new discovery in *DES*. But each site has a correct Gaelic name, so the numbering system should be considered a convenience for non-Gaelic speakers. In the 'catalogue' of sites following, I have included brief summaries of several new studies undertaken since 1984.

No-one knows if the various sites are of similar date, or if they were

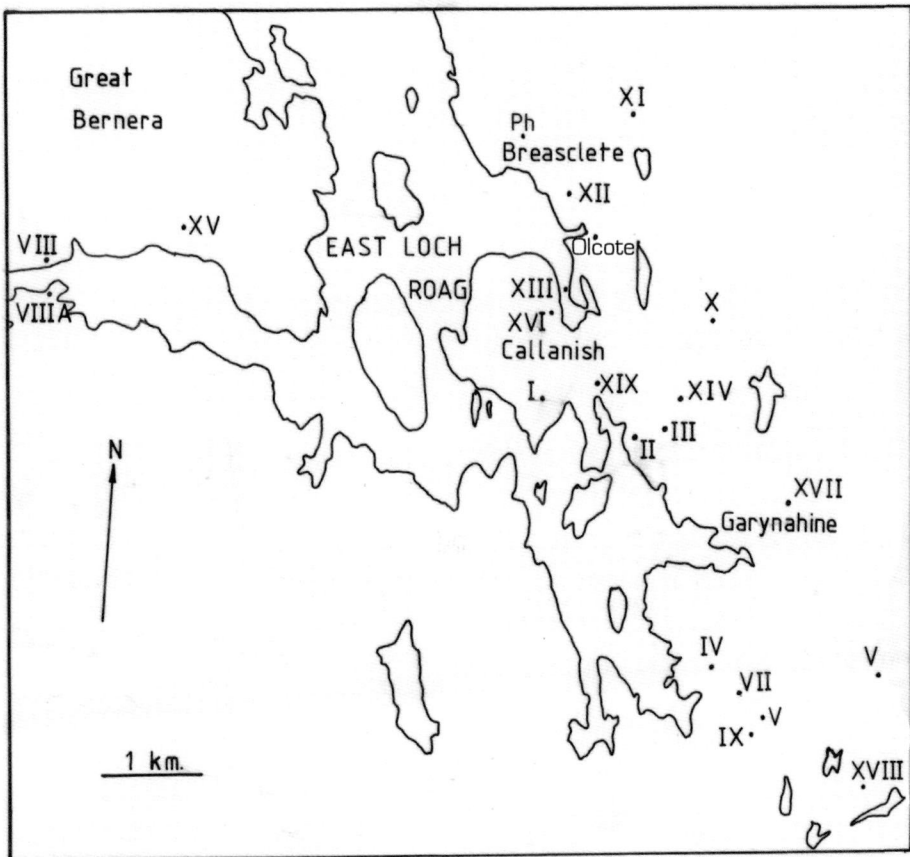

Plan of the Callanish area showing positions of numbered megalithic sites, also the Olcote cairn and Cnoc a' Phrionssa (Ph).

in use concurrently. Nor do we know if they were used by different communities … or indeed different 'sects' of a supposed prehistoric religion. However, we started to refer to the sites collectively as the 'Callanish Complex', using this phrase in the titles of two conference papers (chapters 19 and 20). One of our projects was to assess the intervisibility of sites – standing at one site it was frequently possible, with good eyesight on a clear day, to spot other sites across the landscape.

The idea of the complex was developed by Margaret and Ron Curtis into the concept of a 'sacred landscape'. Archaeologists now prefer the less emotive term 'ritualised landscape' for the Callanish area. The term is also applied to the Kilmartin valley in Argyll, to the Clava Cairns near Inverness, to the 'Heart of Neolithic Orkney', to the Boyne Valley in Ireland and, of course, to the many sites in the Stonehenge landscape. (See chapter 62.)

Cnoc Ceann a'Ghàrraidh - Callanish II

The nearest circle to the main site. One stone was removed in the 19th century, as explained in chapter 17. In 2021 a geophysical survey was undertaken here and at site III by Richard Bates' team; detailed results are awaited.

Cnoc Fillibhir Bheag - Callanish III

There are nine stones standing in a ring, with four others within the ring and some fallen. A group of artists took a great interest in site III in 1980 (chapter 18). Three stones are said to represent 'aspects of the triple goddess – Maiden, Mother and Crone' – with another representing 'the male principle'. On a stormy day in the winter of 1984, the band Ultravox, hoping to follow up their massive hit 'Vienna', recorded their video here for 'One Small Day'.

Sròn a'Chail - Callanish IV (aka Ceann Hulavig)

In the 1970s, this was accessible only by climbing a barbed-wire fence; now there is a gate and a path. Five stones, coated with hoary lichen, stand in a damp hollow, only a minimal amount of peat having been cleared in 1858. One of my most magical memories while studying the Callanish complex was standing alone in this ring at 6:30 on a March 21st morning – the Spring Equinox. Silence and mystery pervaded as the sun rose from a hillside near Achmore, like a ball of fire into a clear sky.

Cnoc Dubh - Callanish VII and *quartz quarry*

Cnoc Dubh is not far from the roadside, south-west of Garynahine, on the opposite side from Ceann Hulavig. Professor Thom was probably incorrect in considering stone structures here to have a prehistoric origin.

However, a discovery in 2002 by Torben Ballin resulted in the application of the same name to a nearby rockface. A twelve-metre-long vein of quartz was shown to have been worked as a quarry in prehistoric times. Remarkably it is in a position that roughly lines up with sites I, IV and V. Quartz tools and flakes have been found in excavations at Brie, Barvas, Callanish, Dalmore and Olcote, some of which may have been sourced from this quarry.

Airigh nam Bidearan - Callanish V
Cùl a Chleit - Callanish VI
Druim nam Bidearan - Callanish IX
Loch Crogach - Callanish XVIII

These four sites require trekking across the moor from Cnoc Dubh. At site V, a row of three stones and a boulder line up with the 'knees' of the Sleeping Beauty and a glimpse of the rising moon at its most southerly. Site VI, with two impressive standing stones and other prone slabs, is probably the remains of a chambered cairn. Site IX consists of a relatively modern cairn and some fallen slabs, which may or may not have a prehistoric origin. Site XVIII is a stone fixed in an upright position, not necessarily in ancient times.

Barraglom - Callanish VII (aka *Cleitir*)

This is a unique site adjacent to the bridge connecting Great Bernera to the Isle of Lewis. Four tall megaliths stand in an approximate semi-circle, the diameter of which is a sheer cliff face above an inlet of the sea. Two of the stones were re-erected on the instruction of the landowner in the late 1980s, followed by a series of rescue excavations by Margaret and Ron Curtis.

Iarsiadar – Callanish VIIIA

Professor Thom, describing Callanish VIII, wrote *'Across the narrows on the Lewis side is (or was) a single stone'*. I knew it as a boulder, forlorn on a grassy verge, where it had apparently lain since a minor road was widened. In August 1999, a team of volunteers led by the Curtises re-erected it, though about ten metres from its assumed original position.

Na Dromannan - Callanish X

The name means 'the backs'. Known incorrectly as Druim nan Eum since its record in the 1928 Inventory, we established the correct name on the advice of Gaelic-speaking neighbours. A cliff face just west of, and lower than, this site may have been the source of the megaliths at the main site.

The Calanais Virtual Reconstruction Project, led by Dr (now Professor) Richard Bates of the University of St Andrews, scanned every stone at site X and created a virtual 3D model. While all of the stones are prone, some have packing stones nearby, so they were almost certainly erect originally. The model shows them standing – and a visitor to the project's website can take a virtual walk around the circle.

Airigh na Beinne Bige - Callanish XI

A single stone stands on a hillside, with a view over the whole Callanish area. It was obviously always known to the people of Breasclete. In fact we were told old tales of stones being removed for use as lintels, towed down to the village on sledges when the ground was frosty or snow-covered*. The site was first mapped and numbered by the Glasgow

---

* It is my personal theory that the great megaliths of Stonehenge and other sites were most likely moved when winter ground conditions were suitable for them to slide easily. Also, this is a time of year when a labour force could more easily have been spared from agricultural activities.

From Callanish XI there is an excellent view over the whole area. The red oval indicates the position of the main site, beyond Callanish village.

geographers. Our entry in *DES* 1976 first brought it to the attention of archaeologists.

Site XI was also investigated by Dr Bates' Project, resulting in national and international headlines – most of which inaccurately implied that the research was at the main Callanish site. The sensation was due, not to geophysical evidence that the stone was once part of a circle, but to evidence for a lightning strike at the centre – *'a massive star-shaped magnetic anomaly'*. There was inevitable speculation – did the stone circle attract the lightning? was the circle constructed to commemorate a spectacular event? Dr Bates wondered if *'the forces of nature could have been intimately linked with everyday life and beliefs of the early farming communities on the island'*.

Stonefield - Callanish XII

When a small housing estate was built in Breasclete in the 1960s, this stone was retained in its original position, but surrounded by a modern plinth – and the houses were named Stonefield.

Callanish XII – a very 'domesticated' megalith at Stonefield, Breasclete.

Sqeir nan Each - Callanish XIII

First recorded by us, this thin slab of rock lies on a shoreline near Callanish village. Joanna Hambly's 2021 survey (chapter 26) believed it to be a natural feature.

Cnoc Sqeir na h-Uidhe - Callanish XIV

In the course of our searches for additional sites, we came across this upright stone. It is only around half-a-metre high but is fixed in place with packing stones. It is visible from about 1.5 km *due east* of the main Callanish site, so in line for equinox sunrise (see box on opposite page).

Airigh Mhaoldònich - Callanish XV

A crofter in Kirkibost, knowing our interests, showed us this large prone megalith on his croft. We believe that it was once erect, as a writer in 1819 mentioned *'Solitary stones ... of a monumental nature ... on the island of Bernera'*. It would have stood three-and-a-half metres tall. For our

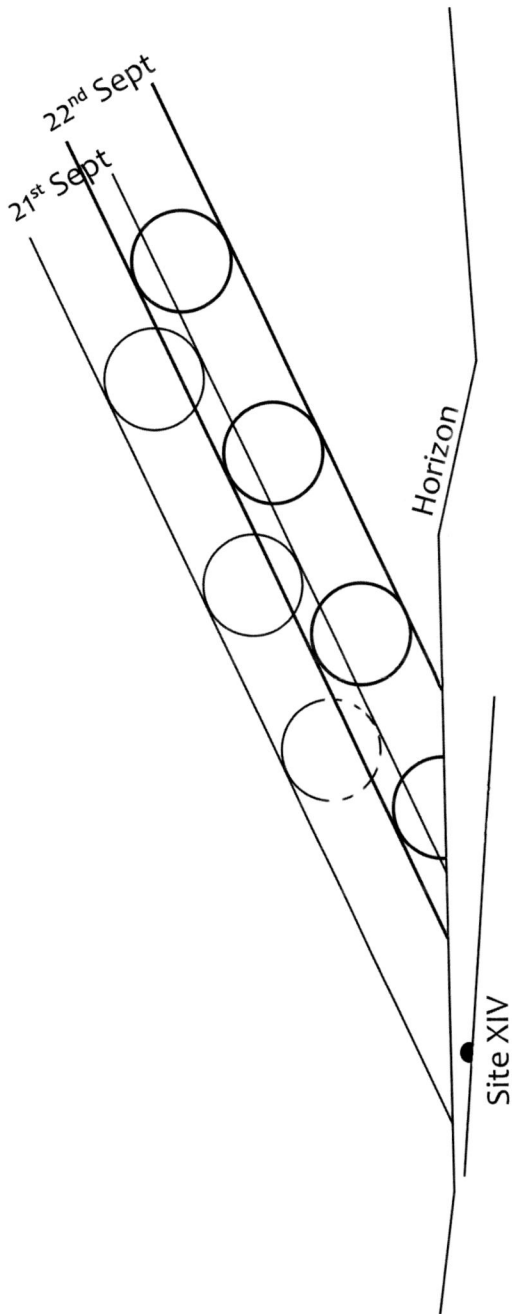

Many researchers think it unlikely that ancient peoples were interested in, even aware of, the equinoxes. Nevertheless, on September 21st 1977, I set up my tripod within the circle at the main site, ready to photograph the sunrise at ten minutes past seven. Unfortunately there was a bank of cloud on the horizon, so the sun appeared later and higher in the sky. When I repeated the experience on the following morning, the sun rose out of a clear horizon. I traced sequences of photographs from both days. The resulting diagram shows that the equinoctial sun would have risen directly above site XIV; and that on the next day, the sunrise was almost a solar diameter further south.

intervisibility project, with permission we erected a tall and conspicuous pole in its place and, as we had expected, found that it would have been visible for miles around.

Cliacabhaigh - Callanish XVI

It is remarkable that no note had been taken of this distinctive one-metre-tall megalith before we first recorded it. Standing near a village house, it is 800 metres north (*almost due north*) of the central stone of Callanish itself. We considered that it must have been deliberately positioned as an outlier of the main site.

Druim na h-Aon Chloich - Callanish XVII

We asked a Gaelic-speaking neighbour to look for significant names on a detailed map. As this name means 'the ridge of the one stone', we explored the slope near Garynahine and discovered a prone, broken megalith. Later, we found a mention in a 1933 travel book, *'The Haunted Isles'*, of a standing stone which *fell on its face some years ago'* during peat cutting.

Buaile Chruaidh - Callanish XIX

A small stone within Callanish village, which appears to be the broken stump of a much larger megalith.

Callanish XVII. The broken megalith on Druim na h-Aon Chloich (the ridge of the one stone) may have been one-and-a-half metres tall when erect.

Standing at Callanish XVII, looking towards the hills of North Harris to observe the most southerly moonset, the stones of Ceann Hulavig / Callanish IV were just visible – boxed on this image. The setting moon, having disappeared behind Mullach an Langa (left of picture), re-appears in the deep notch of Glen Langadale. The moon would finally set behind Teilesval (right) … in direct alignment with site IV. The sloping line has been added to show the moon's path, which would have been a little lower in the Neolithic. Image © B. Ponting.

Cnoc Gearraidh Nighean Choinnich

Discovered by the Curtises in 2001 in the croftland of Breasclete, four prone megaliths remain of what was once a circle of up to fifteen. It seems likely that others were taken as lintels for blackhouse doorways.

Olcote burial cairn

The house where I lived for nine years is called Olcote. I sometimes tethered our goats on a roadside verge just north of our home where they could browse on the wild plants. Little did I know that a burial chamber lurked beneath the soil, a few feet away! The discovery was made in 1995 when preparations were made for widening the road. Sadly, following detailed excavation, the road widening went ahead as planned and only half of the cairn was preserved as a visible monument.

If the line of the avenue at Callanish I is extended by 900 metres across the countryside, it directly lines up with this cairn. Also, the entrance passage of the cairn is oriented directly towards Callanish, further linking sites in the 'Callanish Complex'.

Achmore Stone Circle (chapter 22) has been recorded as Callanish XX, but I consider it too far from the other sites for this to be appropriate.

CHAPTER 17

THE TALE OF A WANDERING MEGALITH

Visitors who take a short detour from the main road at Callanish to find Cnoc Ceann a' Gharraidh (Callanish II) will see five tall megaliths standing in an arc. Studying plans and drawings from the 1850s, made after about three feet of peat had been cleared from around the stones at the direction of Sir James Matheson, it is plain that there was once much more to be seen.

The 'bird's eye sketch' in an 1858 paper by John Stuart is quite remarkable, when one remembers that it was drawn long before anyone had seen an aerial photograph. However, it seems probable that Stuart never visited the site, basing his illustration on an earlier sketch made by Sir James. In addition to the five standing stones, two are shown lying; they are still there today, almost grown over by turf. A much shorter eighth stone stood just in front of the most northerly stone; it must have been beneath the peat before the clearance. There is no trace of it today.

Within the circle there was a cairn and four stone-lined pits. At the time, they were thought of as wells, altars or fireplaces; today it is thought more likely that they were post-holes. Perhaps wooden pillars complemented the standing stones, or even supported some kind of building — which could have been much earlier or later than the stone circle. Only excavation could answer speculations like these.

John Stuart's paper was titled *Notes of Incised Marks on one of a circle of Standing Stones in the Isle of Lewis*. In addition to the features already

The *'Bird's Eye Sketch of Standing Stones'* from John Stuart's 1858 paper. My arrow indicates the stone considered to have 'incised marks' ... which apparently found its way to Stornoway.

mentioned, his sketch showed a fallen stone, about seven feet long. He suggested that the marks on the stone were man-made, but it is possible that this suggestion came from Sir James and he felt obliged to repeat it.

The editor of the Proceedings volume in which Stuart's paper was published was sceptical, commenting that *these apparently scratched lines represent weathering of the stone*'. Fortunately, we were able to obtain from the NMRS a detailed sketch of the stone. No-one today would claim that the marks were anything other than natural.

However, this does not answer the problem of where the stone is now. This is where the importance of studying *all* of the archive material becomes clear. On another plan of Callanish II, anonymously drawn in 1860, the position of the stone is marked *'Bed of Stone Removed to Stornoway'*. Did Sir James believe that the stone was inscribed with script, and that it was best protected by being kept at Lews Castle?

A second clue comes from another plan, this time of a different circle – Ceann Hulavig aka Callanish IV. A note pencilled on the plan reads *'This stone in 1858 was found to be inscribed with Oghams — it is now at Stornoway Castle'*. But the note is crossed through, with the word *'WRONG'* added in different handwriting! Clearly, the annotation had been intended not for Callanish IV, but for Callanish II. Many people think of archives as dull places — but an exciting find like this makes up for many hours of searching!

So, the next problem was — where in the Castle Grounds did Sir James or his Factor consider a safe keeping-place for a 7-foot by 3-foot megalith? — and is it still there? Thanks to some knowledgeable local people, I think I found the most likely explanation.

In the 1850s, Creed Lodge gateway was the main entrance to Lews Castle, the exit by which the Mathesons' house-guests left by horse-drawn carriage for visits to Callanish. What more likely place to put the 'special stone' than immediately opposite the Creed Lodge gateway as a 'taster' for such expeditions?

My nonagenarian informant told me that, until about 1919, there *was* a stone in this position. It stood about four to five feet high, and leaned slightly. The walls of the Castle Grounds needing repair after neglect during the First World War, workmen attempted to break up the standing stone, intending to use fragments in the repair. They were reprimanded for this. Despite extensive enquiries, I heard of no other 'standing stones' anywhere in the area of Lews Castle in living memory.

I made these investigations in the 1980s. At the time, a rough boulder still lay under the rhododendron bushes, opposite Creed Lodge. Measurement and examination could not settle the question, one way or the other, of whether it is the remains of the stone drawn by Stuart. Personally, I would give short odds that this boulder is the remains of Stuart's 'inscribed stone'.

Today it is only in exceptional circumstances that archaeological relics are moved for their protection. Abu Simnel in Egypt is the obvious example. Nearer at hand, Balbirnie Stone Circle in Fife was moved in its entirety in the 1970s as it was in the line of a new road. This was done under meticulous archaeological supervision, and its new position in parkland is considered delightful.

CHAPTER 18

EARTH ENERGIES AND THE 'LUNATIC FRINGE'

Mystically inclined visitors seem especially interested in Callanish III stone circle, perhaps because the site provides such a clear view of the 'Sleeping Beauty' - which some identify as 'the White Goddess'. The hills about 25 miles away in Pairc, south-east Lewis, form an horizon in the shape of a supine female body. The figure must always have been known to the local populace, many ages before she acquired her Gaelic name of Cailleach na Mointeach – Old Woman of the Moors.

The 'Sleeping Beauty' hills. Mòr Mhonadh forms the figure's 'knees', Guaineamol her 'body' and Sidhean an Airgid her 'face'. I once hiked on the hills of Pairc, and found that her 'nose' is formed by a large and prominent rock outcrop.

Artists at Callanish

In London in 1980, a group of *'impoverished artists and photographers, who did not know each other very well'* were prepared to rough it for a month or more in tents on *'a windswept island far to the north-west'*. The intention of London Calling was to 'monitor' the excavation at Callanish planned for that summer. A leading member of the group, John Sharkey, considered excavation *'… a destructive process likely to damage the earth-energies which are still a latent force within these stone monuments'*.

The artists set up camp near the site, but, despite their intention to keep an eye on the archaeologists, the two groups tacitly ignored one another most of the time. (However, the potential for interaction was the inspiration for my unfinished novel – see chapter 42.) The artists concentrated their attention on Callanish III, also exploring the Pairc hills and making pencil sketches of the Sleeping Beauty's 'anatomy'

A direct result of the artists' time on Lewis was an exhibition of drawings, sculptures, watercolours, poetry, photographs and film. Titled *'Callanish – the Sacred Sites of Lewis, Hebrides'*, it was staged, of all places, in Wells-next-the-Sea. I drove on minor roads through the green Norfolk countryside till I reached a coastline of mud-flats and salt-marshes, where a large brick-and-flint granary had become an arts centre. Among the many Callanish-related artworks, large sketches of individual megaliths hung in a circle, accompanied by lumps of Lewisian gneiss hanging precariously by threads.

Sharkey's introduction to the exhibition gives something of its esoteric flavour: '... *the triad of stones, landscape and lunar aspects were the contours upon which we could superimpose a mass of seemingly inconsequential information so that a number of important aspects became clearer*'.

Archaeologists tend to refer to such groups as part of the 'lunatic fringe'. Glyn Daniel wrote that their views were not '*an amusing whimsey to be disregarded ... one of the tasks of archaeology in the 1980s is to see that the lunatics are exposed...*'. Nevertheless, fringe ideas remain popular among those with an imaginative outlook, perhaps put off by the specialist approach of modern archaeology.

Archaeologists admit that they cannot answer the question 'Why?'. We cannot know the motives of our distant ancestors. Why did people settle here? Why was such an imposing temple constructed at Callanish? ... If archaeology cannot answer these questions, the geomancers and their friends are glad to oblige, with theories blended from legends, Celtic myths, 'psychical inspiration' and sometimes pure fiction. It is an area where assumptions rapidly become dogma and the meanings of words are difficult to focus. Sample sentences:

- '... *sacred sites . ... throughout Britain set up a network of communication, through an understanding of vital forces of life which act as a starting-point for universal enlightenment ...*'
- '*Stone circles are part of the polishing process of the human mirror.*'
- '*Stone circles like those at Callanish can be a physical starting point where the White Goddess can be invoked in order to stimulate living forces towards universal harmony*"

Umm!

There are those who claim that the ability to erect megaliths was an engineering skill inherited from the fabled Lost Continent of Atlantis.

Equally denigrating of prehistoric human ingenuity are those writers who claim that Man's best ideas were imparted by alien astronauts — handing us civilisation from a flying saucer!

Returning our attention to the Norfolk gallery, at the far end the eye was drawn to a large representation of Callanish III in relation to the horizon. Coloured lines represented energy flows both within the circle and in the surrounding landscape, lines that the artists claimed to have discovered by dowsing.

Dowsing

Professional dowsers can produce verifiable results when searching for water or prospecting for oil, but it's more difficult to confirm supposed patterns of energy. Dowsing is comparable to acupuncture, a practice that can be very effective in the right hands, yet with no accepted scientific basis.

In the late 70s, a documentary on dowsing at Stonehenge became a staff-room talking point among Nicolson Institute science teachers. The film showed divining rods apparently reacting to the megaliths at Stonehenge. The equipment used was so simple that it was not long before someone came up with the idea of trying it for ourselves at Callanish.

Method: bend part of a metal clothes hangar into an L-shape. Remove the refill from a ballpoint pen and thread the short section of the L through the tube. Hold the pen tube loosely as a handle, the long section of the L pointing horizontally away from the body. In this way, the rod is free to swing left and right independently of the 'operator', showing the 'detection of energy'. Try it with one rod, or with one in each hand.

So, on a subsequent weekend, several of us met at Callanish with our newly-made equipment. We walked around outside the circle. The rods swung towards one stone as we passed it, then away from the next one – great excitement. I then tried walking down the east side of the avenue – swing towards one stone, away from the next. I was excited to get a similar reaction where there was a gap between the stones … my first thought was that *the rods are detecting the positions of lost stones!* However, the thrill did not last long when I realised that the rods were pointing to the fence posts alongside the site! So this was a piece of 'research' which I never followed up!

Dragon Project

In the 1970s and 1980s there were attempts to record supposed earth energies scientifically. The Dragon Project, led by Paul Devereaux, took readings in stone circles using both Geiger counters and ultrasonic detectors. A team spent a week on Lewis in June 1983, taking readings at Callanish, at sites II and III and at Achmore. Their raw data showed no anomalies and, as far as I can discover, no analysis was published. However, other sites showed interesting results.

Merry Maidens in Cornwall is a circle of nineteen granite stones within a granite landscape. Inexplicably, radioactivity levels recorded within the circle were *lower* than in the surroundings. And at Rollright in Oxfordshire, the stones emitted pulses of ultrasound around dawn, more strongly at the equinoxes. So, just maybe, there are measurable energies!

Commenting on such findings, a writer in the Guardian suggested that *'From Lands End to the Western Isles, prehistoric sites chatter away to each other ...'*, then, echoing Shakespeare's *'... more things in heaven and earth ...'* quotation, commented *'... there's more mystery surrounding these prehistoric stone circles than was ever dreamt of by respectable scientists'*.

Although I have always considered myself a practical person, I have to admit that, in the weeks after the *'destructive process'* of excavation at Callanish, the site felt 'dead'. It was some months before the Stones regained their aura of mystery.

CHAPTER 19

PRESENTING OUR 'SOUTHERN MOON SKIM' THEORY

Early on a Sunday morning in March 1980, I was in a lecture theatre at the University of Newcastle, checking slides and equipment prior to giving a lecture at the first national Conference on Archaeoastronomy. It was an opportunity to present our findings to the experts in the field, notably our theory about the 'southern moon skim'.

As this was in the school holidays, I had not needed time off, but with our children spending the weekend with friends in Yorkshire, and Margaret travelling separately from me, we each had copies of a complex 'family timetable' for the weekend! When I arrived alone in the centre of Newcastle, I soon *felt in alien territory in the overheated disco-filled shopping centre*. Obviously I had become accustomed to the relative simplicity of Stornoway town centre. (My return journey included one night in Edinburgh and one in Inverness, where I gave a talk on Callanish to the Inverness Field Club.)

The conference started on Friday evening, when we met and chatted to Aubrey Burl (author of the definitive book on stone circles), Archie Thom (Prof. Thom's son and colleague), Clive Ruggles (academic archaeo-astronomer), John Wood (author of *'Sun Moon and Standing Stones')*, and Gordon Moir (organiser of the conference) .

They were all in our Sunday audience, along with other astronomers and archaeologists. The title of our presentation was *'Decoding the Callanish Complex – Some Initial Results'*. We outlined our discovery of previously unrecorded standing stones in the Callanish area.

Most of our paper was devoted to demonstrating alignments with possible astronomical indications. Over the previous years we had drawn up many diagrams of different solar and lunar events, using the method as outlined in the box.

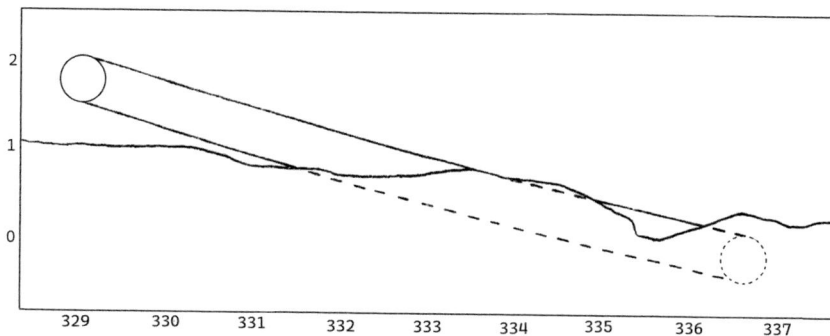

To produce this diagram:

- I set up my tripod at Callanish I, looking north-north-west along the flat face of stone 8, towards an obvious 'notch' in the hills.

- From this point I took a series of photographs of the horizon.

- Margaret used a theodolite from the same position to measure altitude and azimuth at points along the same horizon.

- We traced my photos and added the measured values. *The vertical scale shows degrees of altitude with zero representing a level horizon, while the horizontal scale shows degrees of azimuth: 0 = north, 90 = west, 180 = south, 270 = east.*

- We used a hand-held scientific calculator (long before the days of home computers) programmed with astronomical formulae.

- We drew in the calculated position of the moon, setting at its most northerly position in prehistoric times.

- The result shows an obvious 're-gleam' in the notch, suggesting that the orientation of the stone may have been intended to indicate this moonset.

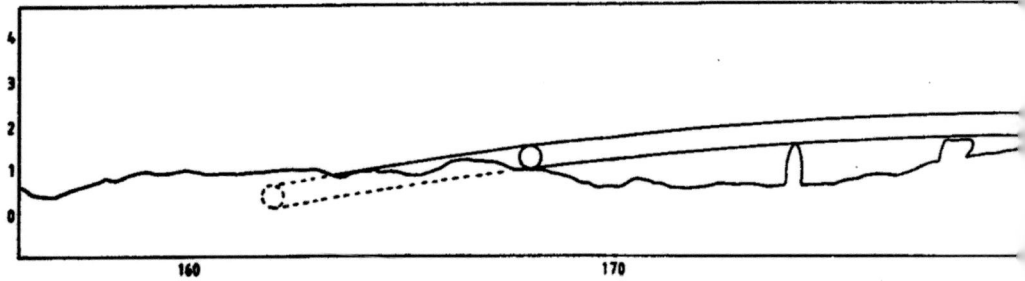

A reduced copy of our moon skim profile, originally drawn on a lengthy sheet of specialist tracing paper. Projected during our lecture, it shows the profile of the southern horizon, including the stones, as seen from the north end of the avenue. The arrow indicates the narrow space to the left of the tall central stone where the moon briefly gleams before finally setting.

We were most interested in the moon skimming across the horizon when travelling its most southerly path – which it does only at intervals of 18.6 years (correctly but a little confusingly called the *'southern extreme of Major Standstill of the moon'*). The importance of this event at Callanish had been hinted at by both Thom and Hawkins, but neither had been able to follow up on the idea.

We used our method described to draw up the horizon profile above.

Projecting this in our lecture, we explained "... *It will be seen that, at the southern extreme of the major standstill at this latitude, the path of the moon traced a spectacular course through the southern sky. ... The moon skimmed over the southern horizon for only about 2 hours between rise and set.*

"*With most of the Clisham range hidden by the site and the rock outcrop, the moon rose out of the 'Sleeping Beauty', skimmed the stones of the east row and set into the stones of the circle. To the left of stone 29, the tall central megalith, the moon briefly gleamed again within the bounds of the circle before finally setting.*

"*Were the avenue lines set out deliberately to give a symbolic descent of the moon into the circle or the central cairn? Was this a ceremonial version for the common people of an event which was of great interest to an astronomer priesthood?*"

84

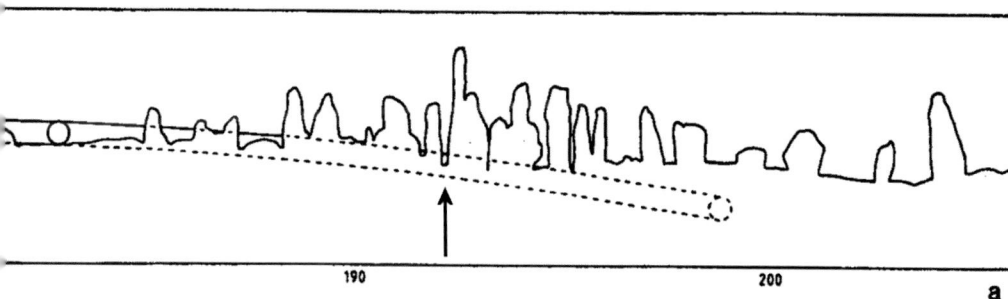

A version of our horizon profile featured in several books, with the moon's southerly path simulated in television documentaries. Somehow, over the years since, the idea has taken on a life of its own, so that our 1980 speculation now appears to many as established fact. Many interested people made critically timed visits to the site in 1987, 2006 and 2025.

the Moon rises gently from Cailleach na Mointeach   passes low at due south, skims some stones of the east row   dips into Cnoc an Tursa   disappears then RE-GLEAMS briefly within the circle at the foot of the largest stone and at the head of the burial cairn

After being adapted in Julian Cope's popular tome *The Modern Antiquarian*, this version of our moon skim diagram appeared in a brochure for the Callanish exhibition held at An Lanntair in Stornoway in 1995. Image © B. Ponting.

On an 18.6 year cycle, clearly the actual 'standstill', the uttermost southerly path, occurs in varying months. However, the moon skims almost as far south in prior and subsequent months, and is best viewed at full moon. The iconic photographs on the next two pages were both taken on nights of the June full moon.

Clive Ruggles wrote, in 2024: '... *a sighting of the moon skimming along the southern horizon – a rare occurrence – would have been a*

On a return visit to Lewis in 2006, I photographed the moon rising out
of the body of the Sleeping Beauty hills at 12:20 a.m. on June 12th.
I have had many publication requests for this photograph.

*spectacular and awe-inspiring event remembered and revered over the gener-
ations ..'* and might have caused *'... such awe and veneration that people
were motivated to memorialise the event in stone'*. But alignments were
*'very unlikely to have arisen because ancient Britons were meticulously
monitoring moonrises or moonsets'*. This leaves no need to suppose, with
followers of Professor Thom, that the ancients actually understood the
long-term lunar cycle.

Those fortunate enough to be at Callanish on the night of June 11th 1987 experienced the 'awe-inspiring moment' when, viewed from the north end of the avenue, the setting moon reappeared briefly within, as it were, the circle of stones. In ancient times, the moon would have been a little lower in the sky than it appears today.

Photographed by Margaret, this image appeared on the cover of *Current Archaeology* and was also reproduced by the *Griffith Observer* of Los Angeles. Image © B. Ponting

CHAPTER 20

INTERNATIONAL SYMPOSIUM
AT OXFORD UNIVERSITY

Following the success of the national conference in Newcastle, the following year (1981) an International Archaeoastronomy Symposium was held in the impressive surroundings of Queen's College, Oxford. With around seventy invited delegates, it was an opportunity for those of us interested in British megaliths to meet, for the first time, researchers from the USA and elsewhere who were studying the astronomical traditions of, for example, the Babylonians, the Mayans and Native Americans of the Hopi, Chumash and Pawnee peoples.

Attending in term-time was something of a problem for me, but the prestige of attendance at an international event must have inspired the Stornoway authorities to allow me time off, and even to assist with travel costs, despite the fact that the topic was unrelated to the subject I taught. However I had to be away from my classes for the minimum amount of time. I taught my lessons on a Friday morning, took two flights, a coach and a train to arrive in Oxford at 9:20 p.m., before walking to the college.

On Saturday, Sunday and Monday, there were presentations by many expert speakers, including Evan Hadingham. A couple of years later, it was my pleasure to write a review for the *Stornoway Gazette* of his new book, *'Early Man and the Cosmos'*. The book hardly mentioned Callanish but, inspired by the Symposium, the author tried to give an insight into the intentions of those who built ancient structures, worldwide, with astronomical connections.

Evan described how movements of the sun and moon were used as the basis of a calendar in different cultures across the world and in different time periods. In previous writings, he had been a supporter of Professor Thom's theories, but with further study, he had changed his mind, having found no evidence that ancient 'astronomers' understood the mysteries of celestial motion.

At British megalithic sites, as in other parts of the world, our ancestors had a unifying vision. Evan wrote that beliefs about the sun and the moon were inextricably linked with the timing of sowing and harvest, the fertility of domestic animals, ceremonies for births, marriages and deaths, and communication with ancestral spirits.

Or, as I later succinctly put it in *'Callanish'* (2000), ' ... *'Primitive' cultures tend to combine all aspects of their lives, including religion, art, medicine, astronomy and farming in a single ritual framework'.*

Of the American speakers at the Symposium, I was especially interested by Anna Sofaer's story of her research at Chaco Canyon in New Mexico. The Anasazi Puebloans aligned many large buildings on solar or lunar directions. But it was the 'Sun Dagger' phenomenon that really impressed me. At the summer solstice, a 'dagger' of sunlight shines precisely across the middle of a petroglyph, a spiral carved into a rock surface. At the winter solstice, *two* daggers of light lie at the exact edges of the same spiral. This clearly shows that a supposedly unsophisticated society really was capable of *accurately* recording astronomical events.

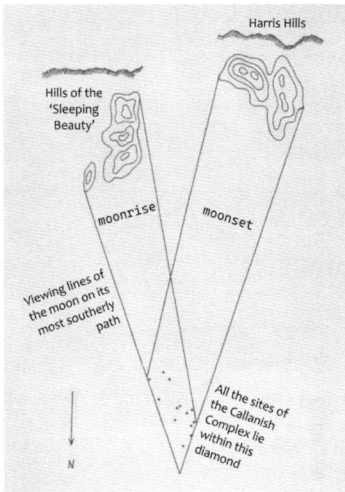

Our own paper was again titled *'Decoding the Callanish Complex'*, this time with the subtitle *'A Progress Report'*. We reiterated the importance of the moon skimming over the horizon when on its most extreme southern path. We introduced a diagram that we called the Callanish Diamond. This indicates that, for *all of the sites* in the Callanish area, the southernmost moon appears to rise from the hills of Pairc in SE Lewis (the 'Sleeping Beauty') and to set into the North Harris hills, often 're-gleaming' in a deep valley between hills.

We had found sites beyond the Diamond, from which the southern moon skim would be visible, though over different ranges of hills and presented our information on Clach an Tursa (next chapter). We also made the point that no modern archaeological studies had been made of any of the 'minor sites' and that it was not known if the many sites were contemporary.

Our presentation was appreciated by the international audience – and resulted in invitations for me to give talks on Callanish in the USA (chapter 57).

On the Tuesday of the Symposium, there was an excursion for delegates and their partners. Richard Atkinson, who had excavated at Stonehenge in the 1950s and 1960s, gave us an expert tour of the site, here explaining one of the Station Stones. At Avebury, Aubrey Burl was our equally knowledgeable tour guide.

On Wednesday, I had breakfast in Oxford, and was back teaching in Stornoway in the afternoon, thanks to a shared taxi from the Oxford college to the Heathrow terminal. Margaret had more leisurely journeys there and back.

CHAPTER 21

CLACH AN TURSA, CARLOWAY

One of the lesser-known megalithic sites on Lewis is Clach an Tursa, situated within the croftland of Carloway. It was first mentioned in print by Martin Martin in 1703 – *'There are three erected Stones upon the North side of Loch-Carlvay, about 12 foot high each. Some of the ignorant Vulgar say, they were Men by Inchantment turn'd into Stones: and others say, they are Monuments of Persons of Note kill'd in Battel'*.

When Dr Callander visited for the RCAHMS in 1914, the site apparently looked much as it did when we studied it in 1981. The two prone and broken stones were probably once taller than the one still erect, which is around 2.3 metres tall. Our measured survey was included in our Oxford conference paper.

The two stones had fallen at some point since 1700, or perhaps more likely were felled. One imagines a deliberate desecration of a 'pagan' structure, but with one stone left standing, just in case the ancient beliefs were valid after all. The position of the fallen stones suggests that the three stones originally formed an alignment, a straight row, but it was impossible to confirm this.

The name Clach an Tursa is of interest – stone of sadness. To the immediate south of the Callanish Stones is a natural rocky outcrop with a similar name – Cnoc an Tursa – hillock of sadness. About three km to the west of Clach an Tursa, not far from the headland of Aird Lamishader, there is a large cuboid stone called Clach Marathain, stone of fortune. It is a natural rock, and not visible from Clach an Tursa, but the contrasting names are interesting.

We did calculations to discover if, when the moon skims the southern horizon, this event could also have been viewed from Clach an Tursa.

The stones of Clach an Tursa within the croftland of Carloway.

These showed that, an hour or two after it rose, it would disappear for a while behind Beinn Iobheir and reappear before it finally set. (This assumes a probable lower ground level at the site in earlier times.) On the summit of Beinn Iobheir (Ivor's Hill) stands a Jubilee Cairn from 1897. Local tradition says that celebrations, sometimes with bonfires, had been held on the hill from time immemorial.

Other Megalithic Sites

About 15 miles north-east of Carloway stands Baile an Truseil / Ballantrushal, a single megalith 5.8 metres tall, probably the tallest in Scotland. Over the years, we visited and photographed many megaliths throughout the Western Isles, but did not have time for any significant research. However, our initial guidebook, '*The Standing Stones of Callanish*', mentioned twelve of them.

My book '*Callanish*' (2002) included brief details of 58 sites, from Clach Stein in Ness to Druim a'

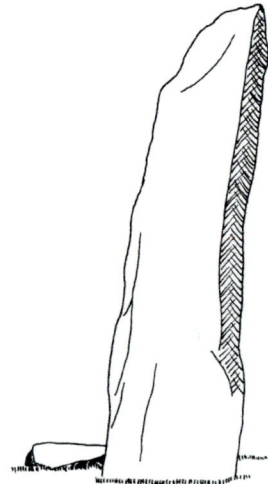

Ballantrushal, while solitary today, was probably once part of, or associated with, a stone circle.

Charra on Barra, earning its subtitle '*. and Other Megalithic Sites in the Outer Hebrides'*.

CHAPTER 22

DISCOVERY OF ACHMORE STONE CIRCLE

Back in the 1930s, John Mackay, cutting his peats on the moorland above Achmore, uncovered a large stone. In subsequent years, as the face of his peat bank retreated, more stones were exposed – a total of eleven over the following 50 years. One was standing erect, though only about one metre tall; all others were prone. He thought that he must be uncovering a stone circle – but his neighbours were sceptical.

In May 1981, with Patrick Ashmore's excavation at Callanish in the news, two local crofters decided to tell us of the possible Achmore site. The five of us went to inspect the area, and Patrick confirmed that it was a prehistoric site ... leaving further investigation to Margaret and myself.

The location of the site was also interesting to us for its view southwards. While the Sleeping Beauty was still visible here, about seven miles from Callanish, another hill formed part of the horizon, making the figure look very obviously pregnant!

With the permission of the landowner, of the local Grazings Committee and of David Maxwell, then working the peat bank, we started to investigate. Initially, we cleared the area around each visible stone, often finding packing stones. I took photographs and we drew a plan of each feature.

Then, using metric tapes and a compass, we did a survey and drew up an overall plan. This showed the stones forming a semi-circle, the existing peat bank forming an approximate diameter. If we assumed an original circular formation, any further stones must, we thought, be under half a metre or more of peat. We plotted the rest of the supposed circle on the uncut surface and hammered in stakes to define it.

Having previously found Stone 33A by probing with a metal rod, we used the same technique. Local youngsters, notably the Campbell boys of Achmore, enthusiastically helped probe the peat around the line marked by the stakes. Each time the rod hit rock rather than soft peat, an excited

ANCIENT STONES UNEARTHED AT ACHMORE

Posed by a press photographer, Margaret is indicating the lower tip of the fallen megalith and the packing stones which once supported it; Benjamin is holding the graduated probe used to detect stones buried in the peat; Rebecca is brushing the stone ready for photography; while the author has a trowel at the ready to expose any more features.
Image © Stornoway Gazette, August 22nd 1981.

cry rang out and a more distinctive stake was used to mark the spot. Eight buried features were found by this method.

Thus David's peat bank rapidly became an archaeological site that created a lot of interest, both among the local people, who often came up to see what we had found, and in local and national media. We were surprised to have a 'hot news story' on our hands!

A senior pupil at the Nicolson Institute drew a clever and amusing cartoon for a school magazine, lampooning me as the bearded rider of an elderly bicycle, apparently creating the Achmore circle by towing megaliths from Callanish! The sketch is signed CMcK; attempts to identify the artist have not proved successful.

The next phase was to reveal the buried features with a series of 'keyhole excavations'. Four of the probed features proved to be groups of packing stones, but the other four were substantial megaliths – exciting finds. Assuming that they were once erect, the largest must have stood almost two metres tall.

Using a theodolite and a more accurate tape, we produced a detailed plan. The site proved to be a true circle, 41 metres in diameter, so one

One of our keyhole excavations in the peat at Achmore, revealing a fallen megalith and packing stones. Inevitably the holes filled with rainwater, leaving only flooded excavation trenches to be seen. Scale – one metre in 10cm sections.

of the largest known in Scotland. A very unusual event, finding a previously unknown prehistoric stone circle.

Our 12-year-old son Benjamin used 'Blue-Peter-style' methods to make a reconstruction model with a polystyrene tile as the base and small plastic cutouts for standing stones, held in place by pins. Photographed with strong side-lighting, this proved remarkably convincing when included in our book *'Achmore Stone Circle'*. We self-published this detailed and fully illustrated 56-page report in December 1981 ... the same year that we had first been told of the possible site. A reviewer in *Popular Archaeology* congratulated us on this promptness and called it, at £2.00, the *'bargain of the year'*.

Our report recorded thanks to the many people who helped in a variety of ways. Our local doctor, John Macrae, produced the text for our report on his electronic typewriter (high tech for the time!) and enthusiastically hired a light plane to provide us with aerial photos. Ron Curtis's sole contribution was establishing an accurate National Grid Reference for the site.

A few years later, the site was officially scheduled as an Ancient Monument. Its details are given in field guides to British stone circles and there is a small parking place with a path leading up to the site. A metal information plaque includes a reproduction of our plan, but does not accurately credit our discovery.

CHAPTER 23

TOTAL LUNAR ECLIPSE
ON A FROSTY EVENING

Anyone who was outdoors on the evening of Saturday 9th January 1982 might have been surprised when a bright moonlit night slowly turned to a dark starry night, while the moon itself took on a deep copper tone. For amateur astronomers, the clear skies that night gave a view of a total lunar eclipse which was near perfection.

Soon after sunset, the full moon rose majestically at the directly opposite position on the horizon. This is the reality behind the textbook diagram of an eclipse, showing the sun, the Earth and the moon in a straight line.

As the moon rose higher in the sky, the snowy landscape around Callanish became bright. The frost was hard, the sky cloudless, but the stars were dimmed by the light of the moon. In the west, the brightest 'star', really the planet Venus, visible as a crescent through our ancient reflector telescope, slowly sank through the remnant pink glow of the sunset, till it winked out on the horizon.

Shortly before 6:30 p.m., a dark 'bite' was taken out of the left side of the moon. To prehistoric man, this must have been an alarming event. Just when the moon shone at its brightest, some mythical sky monster was eating it away! Worse was yet to come, as the dark area gradually spread across the brilliant disc and 'swallowed it up' completely.

Today, we know what is really happening – the moon is passing through the shadow of the Earth, which the sun always casts across space. We even know that the shadow causes the temperature of the lunar surface to plummet by an amazing one hundred degrees Celsius in a few minutes.

When the moon is fully in the Earth's shadow, one might expect it to become invisible against the darkness of the sky. However, the rays of light from the sun are bent as they pass through the Earth's atmosphere. This changes the colour of the light, and gives the darkened moon its distinctly coppery appearance.

As the night became as dark as at new moon, stars appeared in vast profusion and a neighbour's dog howled his alarm at the (for him!) unforeseen event. From 7:17 till 8:35, the moon remained dark. At the latter time, precisely on the timetable calculated by the astronomers, a slim crescent of light appeared at about 'seven-o-clock' on the moon's face. It took almost an hour for this light to spread across, as the moon moved out of the Earth's shadow into its accustomed full sunlight.

As it did so, the dimmer stars disappeared from view, their glow too insignificant to compete with the brighter light. The landscape brightened; across East Loch Roag, we could see the shape of Great Bernera outlined against sea and sky once more, rather than just the yellow 'stars' of the Kirkibost homes glowing in the darkness.

Thanks to clear skies and to the naturally clear air of Lewis, we had been treated to a perfect view of a total lunar eclipse. We gloated slightly when we learnt that Patrick Moore, with the best technology on the roof of the Television Centre in London, had seen nothing due to cloudy skies. A sequence filmed in Birmingham recaptured but poorly the actual experience.

How would prehistoric man have viewed the capture of the 'moon-god' by a mysterious sky monster? Might not the priests have organised ceremonies to appease the monster and to persuade it to give back the valuable light of the night? Their pleas would always have been successful!

Claims have been made that one of the functions of Stonehenge was the prediction of eclipses. I have explained how the placing of standing stones can indicate positions of moonrise or moonset on the horizon. Professor Thom theorised that the timing of eclipses could have been worked out from stone placings without modern scientific knowledge. If the pagan priests of those days could predict eclipses, it would have given them enormous prestige. As evidence mounts for links between Callanish and the movements of the moon, maybe the same applied here.

So, as we watched the remarkable spectacle of an eclipse in the early days of 1982, we thought of our distant forebears of perhaps five thousand years ago watching the same spectacle from the great temple of Callanish. Were they afraid that the moon was gone forever – or were they as confident as we are today that the moon would reappear?

CHAPTER 24

MIDSUMMER SUNRISE

Early morning twilight, midsummer June 1983; a thick haar lay over the land, enveloping the Callanish Stones in eerie grey obscurity. About a dozen people wandered disconsolately in groups. When standing still, they were difficult to distinguish from the stones. With no sign of the hoped-for sunrise, due around 4:20 a.m., people gradually walked or drove away, disappointed after the previous day's clear skies.

About half-an-hour later than the sun's non-appearance at Callanish, and around 600 miles to the south, the sun rose dramatically over the Heel Stone at Stonehenge, into a clear sky. White-robed neo-Druids went about their counterfeit rituals, while 20,000 illegal campers partied in a jam-packed nearby field, the so-called 'Stonehenge Free Festival'. As a student, long before the days of the 'festival', and before I had ever heard the name Callanish, I had once kept the all-night midsummer vigil with some friends at Stonehenge and been rewarded with a perfect sunrise.

A year after the previous disappointment at Callanish, on June 21st 1984, I left my bed at 3 a.m. and, as arranged, picked up a group of senior pupils from Stornoway in the Nicolson Institute minibus. We hoped to see the sun rise at the Stones, but the weather did not look promising. Across the moors and through sleeping Achmore, there was thin drizzle, with a Runrig tape keeping us awake and cheerful.

Arriving at the Stones in darkness at around four o'clock, we found it uncomfortably bleak, with a chill wind sweeping across the site. While there were a few lighter patches in the sky, the horizon to the north-east was totally cloud-covered. We wandered around, joined by Sam Maynard, the *Stornoway Gazette* photographer, and other friends. A couple of tourists had already been waiting an hour, uncertain of the time of sunrise.

Four-fifteen passed, and 4:20, with no sign of the sun, not even a patch of brightness in the sky. However, the clouds were moving rapidly southwards across the eastern horizon. A small area of sky lightened near the spot where I knew that the sun should be. No one believed me when I said that the sun was about to appear.

Suddenly, at about 4:30, the sun emerged in the gap in the clouds. The whole scene lit up dramatically. The clouds glowed gold and purple. Sam immediately started shooting off film; several of us also took out our cameras.

Although we had not seen the actual moment of sunrise, the sun being already a little above the horizon when it appeared, everyone was well satisfied with the experience. The gap in the clouds was a small one, well timed, with the sun remaining visible for only about ten minutes. The beauty of that moment gone, the chill wind made itself felt again and we began to return to the minibus. As we did so, the heavens opened, a sudden downpour, and we ran in confusion from the circle to the parked minibus. As we settled our damp bodies into our seats, someone joked — 'The revenge of the Druids!'.

We had planned to heat a breakfast of sausages on a camping stove — where could we find a sheltered spot away from the bitter wind? After driving north to Carloway, our 'mini-barbecue' took place within the Broch*— another unique and memorable experience!

We returned to Stornoway around seven o'clock, in time to have an

---

* I don't think I should need to point out that using a camping stove, barbecue or similar at the Stones, the Broch or any other protected site would be considered totally inappropriate today.

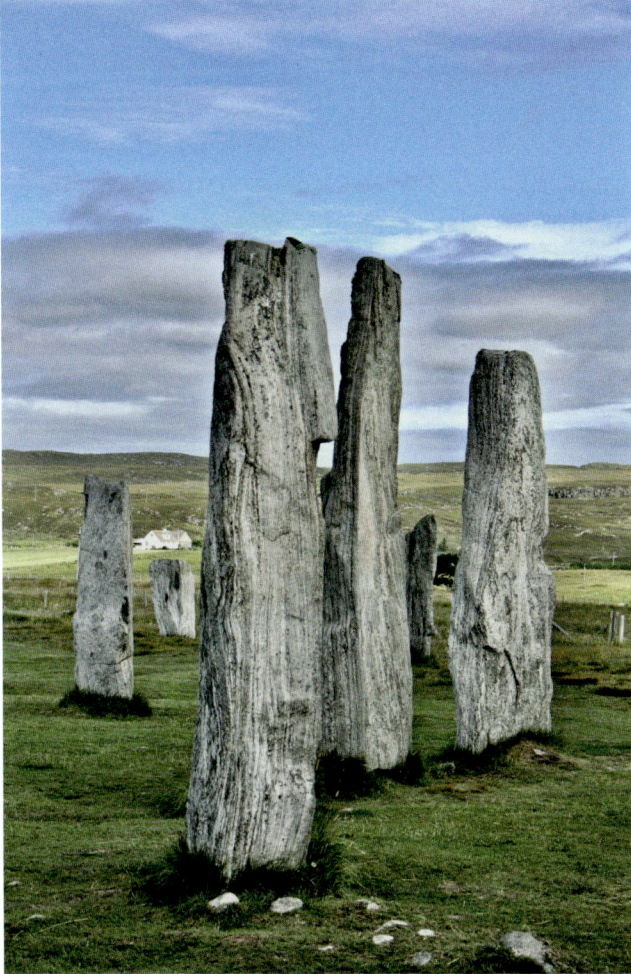

A 'sun window'. If you stand in a precise spot within the circle, so that two stones overlap in your vision, a small squarish aperture is formed. An overhanging projection on stone 51 forms the left and top of the window, while a 'shelf' on stone 52 forms the right and bottom. This could be a coincidence of construction, but once you have spotted the window, it looks deliberate ... and the restricted view is of the *very spot where the sun rises at the summer solstice*. However, it is difficult to imagine its ritual use in a ceremony as it can be viewed only by one person at a time. Image © Laurel Kallenbach (Colorado)

hour's sleep before the start of the school day. But, is there anything special about midsummer at Callanish? Do the few visitors each midsummer morning visit simply because of an imagined Stonehenge connection, while enjoying the solitude of Callanish? There is no equivalent of the Heel Stone indicating the point on the horizon where the sun may appear. However, Margaret spotted a small and intriguing 'window', shown in the box on the previous page.

CHAPTER 25

ICONIC PHOTOGRAPHS OF SUN AND SNOW

In the northerly latitude of Lewis, daylight lasts only around six hours at the winter solstice. One of the corollaries of this was that, during term time in winter, I saw daylight at home only at weekends. In contrast, with 18 hours of daylight in mid-June, on bright summer evenings schoolchildren found it difficult (or were reluctant) to settle to sleep at a suitable time.

Thus it was that, one evening in June 1978, 10-year-old Benjamin, who should have been asleep, dashed downstairs and said – *'Dad, have you seen the sky?'*. I went outside, saw a spectacular formation, shot back inside to grab my camera, then drove quickly to the Callanish Stones. It was about 10:15 p.m. and the sun was low on the north-western horizon, due to set in under half an hour. It was surrounded by a halo – a glowing semi-circle of light. There were brighter areas directly above and horizontally to left and right – formations called perihelia or 'sun-dogs'. I later learned that the phenomenon is caused by light being refracted off ice crystals in a thin veil of cloud.

In these digital days, we can snap away with phone or camera, with no cost for each shot. But in the days of film, when each click of the camera, each resultant colour transparency, had a definite price tag, I probably limited myself to around a dozen shots. For some, I positioned myself so that the sun was directly behind the tallest central megalith, rendering all of the stones in silhouette. It was a very photogenic scene, but also a magical experience, so I soon put the camera aside just to enjoy the lighting as the sun descended.

When, a week or so later, I received the transparencies in the post, I was very pleased with one shot in particular and felt that it was probably marketable.

Today there are several large photographic libraries such as Alamy and Shutterstock, which act as go-betweens for photographers on one hand, and designers of books, magazines and websites on the other. In the 1970s and '80s there were many small specialist libraries, Janet and Colin

Bord operating one focussing on archaeology. I deposited a number of my best transparencies with them, most but not all of Callanish.

Over a period of about eight years, I earned the equivalent of around £5000, even though the Bords took 40% of the income from each sale. The sundog photo was by far the best seller. It appeared in various books, including a double-page spread in *'Cosmic Connections'* from Time-Life – though with poor colour rendition. That sale provided my biggest individual income, but the most prestigious use was wrapped across the front and back cover of Aubrey Burl's paperback, *'A Guide to the Stone Circles of Britain, Ireland and Brittany'*.

My photograph of a sun-halo was reproduced on the first of a set of collectable cards included in packets of PG Tips tea. The colour reproduction was poor and, unsurprisingly, there were errors in the text – Callanish is older, and the photograph was not taken at midsummer sunrise.

Teacard shown at actual size.

A Series of 40 — No. 1

Unexplained Mysteries of the World

Rings of Stone

There are more than 900 stone circles in Britain, built between 3000 and 1200 BC. Though most are ruined, a few have survived, like the most famous of all, Stonehenge. Very little is known about the builders and their purpose, but painstaking work by adventurous archaeologists has shown that the rings have a complicated geometry. Marker stones or prominent natural features were used additionally to compute astronomical events, like eclipses.

Our photograph shows Callanish circle on the Isle of Lewis. Dating back to about 2000 BC, it is one of Britain's most beautiful megalithic sites. This superb picture was taken at a mid-summer sunrise with a spectacular solar halo.

Photograph: Gerald Ponting/Janet & Colin Bord

Save your 40 picture cards in a special album. Just send 2×20p coins plus your name and address to:
Brooke Bond Picture Card Dept.,
PO Box 216, Croydon CR9 3TA

A periodical called *'Stonehenge Viewpoint'* was rather surprisingly published in Santa Barbara, California. It was the brainchild of Donald Cyr, who believed that sun halos were ubiquitous in ancient times, and that the builders of stone circles memorialised them in some form. He was so taken with my sundogs photo that he bought the USA rights for a sum which covered the cost of a new camera. While not in any way supporting his odd theories, we enjoyed spending time with him and his daughter when they visited Lewis. The next issue of 'Stonehenge Viewpoint' contained Donald's long enthusiastic account of our discovery of Achmore Stone Circle.

A couple of years after I took the sundogs photo, snowy windy weather meant that schools were closed for the day. Late in the afternoon, the blizzard had abated and the sun was shining. I took the opportunity to visit the Stones with my camera. As I was the first on site since the storm, the snowy surface was pristine. What is more, the westerly wind

This photograph of the snow-blasted megaliths was used on the cover of '3rd Stone' magazine in 2003. The same issue featured my detailed article about the 'wandering megalith' (chapter 17). My 'fee' for photograph and article was a lifetime subscription to the magazine ... which ceased publication a few years later!

had blasted the snow onto the sides of the megaliths, the sky was blue and the low sun was creating long shadows, a most unusual photographic opportunity.

CHAPTER 26

A CHRONOLOGY OF CALLANISH STUDIES – from 1975

This chapter continues the chronology from chapter 9 and includes points not mentioned elsewhere.

1975   We began our studies of the Callanish Stones*, initially inspired by Professor Thom's first book.

1977   We self-published '*The Standing Stones of Callanish*', the first guidebook to the site.

1977   A paper using a statistical approach to alignments at Callanish was published by astronomy graduates John Cook, Roger Few, Guy Morgan and Clive Ruggles.

1978   We discovered the broken-off tip of stone 19 and it was later glued back in place.

1978   We received a British Archaeological Award and our research was featured in *Current Archaeology* and on BBC1 '*Chronicle*'.

1978   Based on a detailed survey, Glasgow University Geography Department published its large-scale map of the Callanish area

---

* Decades later, journalist John Macleod wrote *"It was only in the Seventies, when two spirited incomers – Gerald and Margaret Ponting – began to make serious, serious study of the Callanish Stones that there was real advance in scholarship".*

with a plan of each individual site. We had used an advance copy to assist in the finding of additional sites.

1980, 82 Patrick Ashmore directed two month-long seasons of excavation at Callanish.

1980 We were invited speakers at a national conference in Newcastle, where we introduced our 'moon skim theory'.

1981 We presented a second paper at an International Symposium on Archaeoastronomy held at Oxford University. (It became the first of a series, with the thirteenth Symposium held in July 2025 in Melbourne, Australia.)

1981 We published '*Achmore Stone Circle*' with a full account of our work at a previously unknown site.

1982 Stone 33A was re-erected in its original position at the east end of the east row, over five years after we had proved its existence beneath the turf.

1983-4 I wrote a series of archaeological columns for the *Stornoway Gazette*.

1984 We published '*New Light on the Stones of Callanish*' and '*The Stones around Callanish*' as replacements for our original guide-book.

1984 Canongate Press failed to publish '*Callanish – Stonehenge of the Hebrides*'. It had been planned as a large popular book based on our privately-circulated academic volumes '*Callanish – the Documentary Record*'.

1984 I gave an illustrated lecture on Callanish at the Smithsonian Institution and at other venues in the United States.

1984 I left Lewis and returned to my home county of Hampshire.

1987 In a year of the moon's major standstill, Margaret was able to photograph the moon setting, apparently within the stones of the circle.

1989 Margaret married Ron Curtis. They continued studying the islands' archaeology, including excavations at Callanish VIII.

1990 The Ordnance Survey introduced the Gaelic spelling 'Calanais', although 'Callanish' was originally derived from Norse.

1990s Several of the minor sites and Achmore Circle were scheduled as Ancient Monuments.

1993 Excavations near Cnoc an Tursa suggested a focus of prehistoric activity on and around this rocky outcrop, possibly before the stones were erected.

1994 Urras nan Tursachan, the Standing Stones Trust, was established and opened the Calanais Visitor Centre the following year.

1995 The official guidebook was published – 'Calanais – The Standing Stones' by Patrick Ashmore

1995 Olcote Cairn was discovered during road widening.

1995 An Lanntair in Stornoway staged a major exhibition, Calanais – the Atlantic Stones.

1999 Clive Ruggles was appointed Professor of Archaeoastronomy at the University of Leicester, showing academic acceptance of the discipline.

2000 Excavations to the south-west of the stones found evidence of Bronze Age agricultural activity (chapter 41).

2002 Wooden Books published my 'Callanish and other Megalithic Sites of the Outer Hebrides'. A small book, it contains the essence of the planned Canongate volume. It remains in print.

2002 A vein of quartz at Cnoc Dubh was discovered to have been used as a quarry in the Neolithic period.

2006 Our moon skim theory of 1980 having become well-known, moon-watchers gathered at the Stones on appropriate nights. On a brief return visit to Lewis, I photographed the June full moon rising from the 'body of the Sleeping Beauty'.

2007 I gave a presentation on Callanish at Megalithomania in Glaston-bury. My talk is still available on YouTube, though audio only.

2013 Ian McHardy first observed the midday sunbeam created by a natural crevice in Cnoc an Tursa.

2013 Colin Richards and associates defined sites in the Callanish area as 'high circles' or 'low circles'. Callanish I, II, II and IV are all sited on low ground and were clearly created as imposing monuments for permanent use. Indeed, most of their stones remain erect millennia later. The stones of the 'high circles', notably Na Dromannan (Callanish X) and Achmore, may have been intended to stand only temporarily, perhaps as waymarkers on a route to the more important low circles.

2016   Patrick Ashmore's much-delayed report on the 1980-81 Callanish excavations was published online by Historic Environment Scotland.

2016   Gail Higginbottom and Roger Clay studied the positioning of stone circles in their landscapes and their possible relationships with the rise and set of sun and moon. Calculating a 'statistical likelihood' that the design of Callanish included astronomical alignments, they found a value very close to 100%. Callanish and Stenness in Orkney were considered the forerunners of such considerations elsewhere.

2017   Duncan Garrow and Fraser Sturt explored crannogs in Lewis lochs. Neolithic pottery found underwater showed that crannogs had been in use earlier than previously thought.

2018   A team from the University of St Andrews scanned the stones at site X and created a virtual reconstruction. They also used geophysics at site XI, revealing that it had been a stone circle, with evidence for a 'massive lightning strike' at its centre.

2021   Joanna Hambly of SCAPE (Scottish Coastal Archaeology and the Problem of Erosion) led a group of local volunteers on a walking survey of Loch Roag coasts near Callanish. They discovered prehistoric field walls under the peat (as well as a piece of struck flint and the remains of former woodland). As the walls were eroding at the high tide mark it is probable that they once continued on what is now seabed.

2021   In a related project, led by Richard Bates, this submerged ancient landscape was examined by sonar survey, while the intertidal zone was surveyed by drone.

2022   My ex-wife's decades of dedication to Callanish, both as Margaret Ponting and as Margaret Curtis, were recognised by detailed obituaries in the national press.

2024   I was interviewed about my Callanish studies by The Prehistory Guys. The resulting video appears on YouTube as *'Calanais Conversations Episode 6'*.

2025   The Calanais Visitor Centre was closed for renovation and enlargement.

2025   18.6 years since 2006, the moon again reached its Major Standstill. Visitors to Callanish hoped to observe the moon on its low southern passage from the Sleeping Beauty to the stones of the circle.

PART 4

Finds and excavations, 1891–1974

———

The chapters in this section are adapted from my *Stornoway Gazette* columns of the 1980s. Most were based on my study of papers which had been published in technical journals.

CHAPTER 27

'TUNNELS' AT GRESS – AND OTHER ODDITIES

The local history collection in Stornoway Library holds an intriguing article, sent as a letter in 1894 to the Secretary of the Society of Antiquaries by the farmer then living at Gress Lodge. Peter Liddell's writing is a strange pot-pourri of unskilled archaeology, folk-lore and superstition. The long title is *'Note of an Underground Structure at Gress near Stornoway and some other Ancient Remains in the Island of Lewis'*. The Gress site also featured in J G Callender's 1914 surveys.

Gress Lodge 'Tunnels'

Describing the *'underground structure'*, Liddell recorded that the first chamber had a roof composed of large flagstones. It may once have been supported by a masonry pillar, but erosion had caused part of the roof to collapse. Split bones and shells of edible molluscs were found in the chamber. Liddell believed that large whelk shells had been used as lamps. He also found quern stones. A *'stag's horn'* was discovered fifteen feet below the floor of the furthest chamber – he clearly did not possess the restraint necessary to a responsible amateur archaeologist!

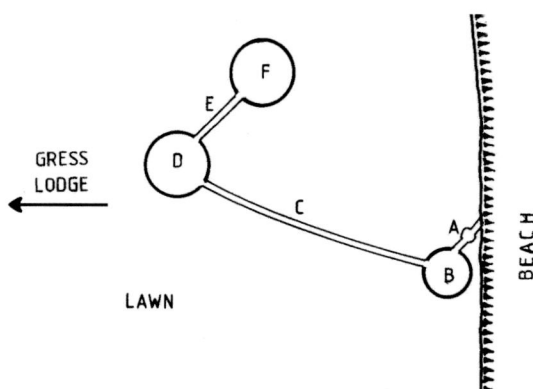

I drew up this guesstimated plan of the tunnels and chambers near Gress Lodge for my *Stornoway Gazette* article in 1984. Callender's entry in the *Inventory* described a long passage leading to a second chamber, with another tunnel to a third chamber. Liddell recorded nine feet as the diameter for chamber B and 40-50 feet for the length of tunnel C, but he gave no dimensions for chambers D and F, nor for tunnel E. Hence my plan is to be taken with a pinch of salt!

Erosion of the sandy cliff continued, encouraged by storms and by the activities of sheep and rabbits. There is nothing left to see, although in 1984 I wondered if a large slab lying on the beach may once have been part of the structure. Today's archaeologists consider the 'tunnels' to have been Iron Age souterrains.

Crannog at Tolsta

The first of Liddell's *other ancient remains* was a crannog (a dwelling on an artificial island) that he claimed to have found at Tolsta, exposed when a loch was drained. A causeway of large stones led to the island on which were the remains of three 'houses'. He recorded finds of wooden piles, five to six inches in diameter, stones and gravel perhaps used in construction. Midden material found on the site included mussels and other shellfish; also bones, mainly of deer and of *'Highland sheep'*.

Recent work in freshwater lochs on Lewis has revealed well-preserved Neolithic pots lying on the loch bed near known crannogs.

Castle Rock, North Tolsta

Liddell evidently climbed to the top of 'Castle Rock' at North Tolsta, finding a stone structure with two chambers. He *'dug all over the floor'*, finding two fireplaces, many hammer stones, and large quantities of *'broken craggans'*. No doubt these were sherds of ancient pottery, which would tell archaeologists a great deal about the site, were they still available.

He found very few bones on the rock *'which may be accounted for by the facilities they had for disposing of them, by throwing them at once over the rock'*!

Serpent Stones

Liddell described several perforated stones owned by local people in the vicinity of Back. Known in local folklore as 'serpent-stones', they were considered effective in curing cattle and people who were 'serpent-bitten'. A strange idea when there are no snakes on the island!

Liddell found one of these serpent stones of particular interest. Round, perforated, semi-transparent, and water-worn, it may have been an ancient amber bead. An old man, Donald Macleod, had obtained it 60 years previously from a very old lady. Its owner was reluctant to allow Liddell even to examine it; he was told that its loss would be a great calamity for the whole district. Believed to have extraordinary curative properties for various ills, the stone was circulated around local villages; and was especially in demand if a 'lesser' serpent-stone had failed to effect a cure.

Snuff Querns

In the vicinity of Gress Lodge, Peter Liddell found snuff querns, once used for grinding tobacco to make snuff. He attributed them to his predecessor, a fish curer, probably before 1800. When cured fish was exported, the ships often returned with raw tobacco … which had somehow avoided the knowledge of the customs authorities!

Wooden Objects Under the Peat

A find made seven feet under the peat, presumably when peat cutting, included a three-stone hearth. Six wooden spoons and four wooden dishes, together with an ox horn, were contained in a box carved from a single piece of wood. These would have been great treasures with modern conservation techniques. The one spoon kept by Liddell would soon have shrivelled away.

A New Discovery in October 1984

Work on a new bridge came to a halt when workmen uncovered a stone-built tunnel. The news story in the *Gazette* mentioned tunnels at Gress Lodge explored by two boys in the 1940s, probably part of the same underground structure known in 1874. Margaret's initial examination of the site by the bridge was followed up by a visit by Niall Sharples. He considered it a cellar of an above-ground house, dated between 700 BC and AD 400. Scotching local rumours, he said that bones found were of animal origin, definitely not human.

CHAPTER 28

THE ADABROCK HOARD
AND DELL SWORDS

When Donald Murray, in 1910, found what became known as the Adabrock Hoard, illustrated in chapter 1, he carefully collected all of the pieces and informed the National Museum of Antiquities, stating that he had found them *'all in one group, the small things above and the heavier below'*, with no sign of a box or bag. However, two bronze fragments have been interpreted as the remains of a large bowl, which perhaps originally held the other items.

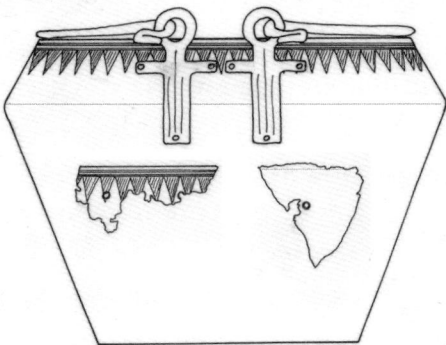

Drawings of two bronze fragments, superimposed on a copy of John Coles' reconstruction drawing. One fragment clearly shows the Hallstatt-style edge decoration, the other suggests the shape of the shoulder. Their curvature suggests a total diameter of about one foot, while both have holes suggesting handle attachments.

The hoard has been dated to the Late Bronze Age, around 950-750 BC. This makes it contemporary with the 'Hallstatt' phase in central Europe, where similar cross-handled bowls have been recovered.

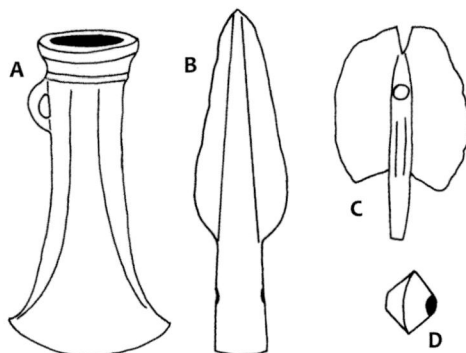

Four items from the Adabrock Hoard – see also illustration in chapter 1.

A – the largest of two bronze axeheads, each with a socket for a wooden handle. B – a spearhead, four-and-a-half inches long, with a deep socket for a wooden shaft. (Other bronze items included a socketed gouge, a tanged chisel and a hammerhead.) C – the largest of three 'razors', each with a tang for a wooden or perhaps bone handle. D – a bead of thin beaten gold, half-an-inch in diameter. While similar biconical gold beads are known from English sites, they are rare in Scotland. Redrawn from John Coles.

In addition to the bronze items, there were two whetstones, used to sharpen cutting edges. As well as the gold bead, there were two beads of amber and one of blue glass, all rare and presumably prized objects.

In his 1914 report on the find, Joseph Anderson concluded – *All the implements are such as have been in use and are still useable, and meant to be kept serviceable by the hammer and whetstones found with them. Five of the tools are for woodwork and three are for shaving, so that the man may have been a travelling wood-worker and barber, and the ornate bronze vessel which seems to have contained the hoard may have been his barber's basin.*

A more modern interpretation, from the website of National Museums Scotland, is that the hoard was *'... an important deposit. The sacrifice of such exceptional and individual objects – many of which must have been difficult to acquire – was probably linked to a significant event.'*

The Aird Dell sword (chapter 1), also loaned to the Ness museum in 2023, was in such good condition that it too was probably 'the sacrifice of an exceptional object'. Remarkably it retained its horn handle with attachment rivets surviving. A few months after finding the sword while peat cutting in 1891, Murdo Macinnes found part of a second sword nearby. It was missing both the top end of the hilt and the lower end of the blade. The deliberate destruction and depositing of weapons is a practice known from across Bronze Age Europe.

CHAPTER 29

THE WEAVER OF SANDWICK HILL

Interesting archaeological specimens sometimes appear in the most unlikely places. At Smith's Shoe Shop, where my 1980s shoe repairs were sometimes accompanied by a yarn on matters prehistoric, I was once asked to *'have a look at some things'* in a back room.

A cabinet was opened and a shoe-box pulled out – what else? The first thing to catch my eye in the box was a piece of bone, shaped into a comb at one end. From its shape, it must have been fashioned from the more-or-less cylindrical central section of an animal leg-bone. Four teeth of the comb were missing but fortunately three were still present.

There were two other man-made objects in the box — or rather, objects that had been modified for a practical use.

The largest item was a flat disc of bone with a hole in the middle, making it useful as a spindle whorl. Prehistoric peoples often span wool by hand, using a straight stick pushed through a disc with a hole in. As the disc span round, hanging from the hank of wool, thread was formed from the hank held in the hand. Years earlier, I had seen this carried out in villages in Turkey — and I can vouch for the fact that it is not an easily-acquired skill! The spinning wheel is, of course, a more sophisticated version of this technology.

Prehistoric spindle whorls in Britain were often made from drilled round stones, or were deliberately fired pottery shapes. The disc in the shoe box was very large for a piece of bone — so large that it must have been part of a whale vertebra.

The third object was an oval beach pebble, with a hole drilled through one end – a loom weight. All sorts of objects were used in prehistory to hold down the vertical threads of an upright loom, with drilled stones a common choice.

Taken together, I found the collection of great interest. The drilled stone was used in weaving; the drilled bone disc in spinning — and the comb was intended for carding wool. All three items might have been used by one individual in the process of making raw wool into cloth. Also, the collection was roughly dateable, as that type of comb was not in use before the Iron Age, which lasted roughly from 800 BC till AD 400 in Scotland. Obviously, I was immediately interested to discover the circumstances under which these fascinating items had been discovered.

During the construction of the runway at Stornoway airport in about 1941, a mound that was part of Sandwick Hill was being bulldozed flat. A stone-lined grave was uncovered — it had remained free from sand for centuries — and the workers were awed to see a skeleton laid out, with the comb and other objects, bones from seal and whale, and some pots.

The general opinion at the time was that it was the body of '*one of the whalers who died in 1880*'. No-one wanted the bother of an official report, so the grave was rapidly covered in; presumably it is still there beneath the runway! But, before the bulldozer concealed the body, many of the objects were removed — and those already described found their way into that shoe-box. The pots may have been retained by other members of the workforce. Had they been available, a firmer date within the Iron Age might have been established.

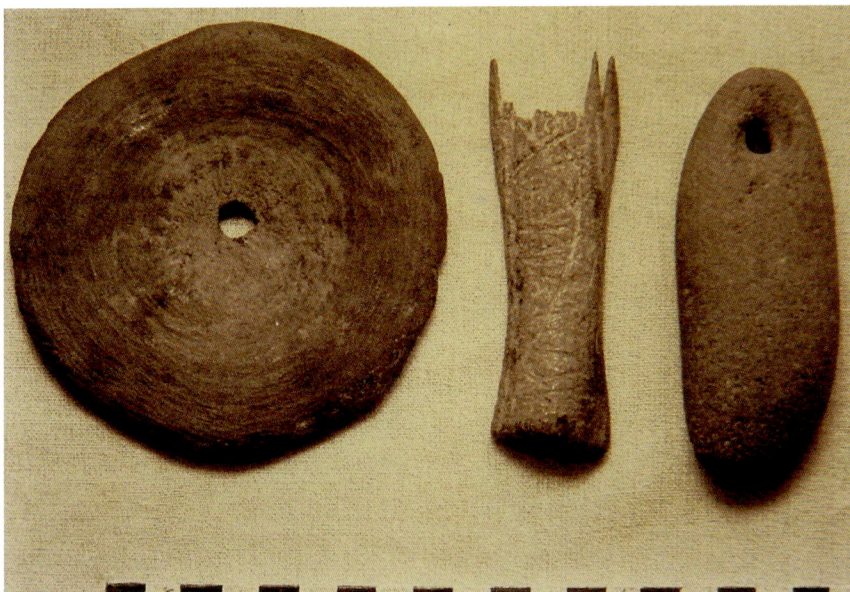

Finds from Sandwick Hill – a spindle whorl of whalebone,
a bone comb with most of its teeth missing, and a pebble
drilled as a loom weight. Scale in cm.

Each time that I had completed one of my archaeology columns,
I handed in my typed pages at the *Stornoway Gazette* office, together
with any drawings or photographic prints. In due course I received
payment, a few pence per line of text and £3.00 for each image
published. When submitting this Sandwick article, I felt that it would
look better on the page with three separate pictures. Not thinking
about payment, I cut the photographic print into three before
handing it in – thus earning £6.00 for two scissor cuts!

I first published this short description of these objects 43 years after
the original find, recording an addition to the known Iron Age finds in
Lewis. I wonder if interesting objects are still held by private individuals,
tucked away in shoe-boxes or other containers. Under Treasure Trove
law, a finder is obliged to report ancient items found in the ground; they

could be of value to archaeologists, especially if the location of the original find is known.

CHAPTER 30

A MEDIEVAL PLAQUE FROM BENBECULA

Caisteal Bhuirgh / Borve Castle was built between 1344 and 1363. As a stronghold of Clan Ranald, it was of great importance locally till the demise of the clans after Culloden. Today, the collapsed walls form an impressive ruin in the south of Benbecula.

About 500 yards to the south west lies a much less impressive ruin, Teampull Bhuirgh. The description of this church in the *Inventory*, based on a visit in 1914, gives its size as 46 feet by 18 feet, but even then the walls were almost covered by sand. There is a tradition that castle and church were connected by an underground tunnel. This is almost certainly unfounded, but traditions of tunnel connections are common to many groups of sites throughout Britain.

In 1943 Mr T Sidwell was stationed in Benbecula, at the RAF base at Borve. At that time only a small fragment of masonry stood above the sand, and Mr Sidwell's curiosity was aroused. He started a small 'excavation' in his spare time, digging a hole about three feet long and two feet wide against a side wall of the chapel. When the hole was about 8 to 10 feet deep he found a black layer that he took to be the floor. Mr Sidwell then continued his excavation in the form of a tunnel alongside the wall. (A modern Health and Safety inspector would be horrified!)

He reached a box-like structure, which he called an 'altar'. It was open

turquoise enamel

deep blue enamel

enamel missing

This bronze medieval religious plaque, shown actual size, was found on Benbecula in 1943.

Enough gilt and coloured enamel remain to make the original design clear. The central feature is the seated figure of Christ with his right hand raised in blessing. Formal patterns and foliage occupy spaces around the figure. Four holes near each of the edges were probably used to attach it to a wooden cross. Such plaques, still attached to crosses, may be seen in museums at Vannes and Le Mans. The two additional holes near Christ's shoulders suggest removal from the cross and attachment to clothing. Photograph © National Museums Scotland / Drawing provided by D H Caldwell.

at one end and the 'box' was free from sand, so he was able to crawl inside ... where he found a skeleton. Various objects accompanied the bones, one of which was perhaps a rusty dagger. The only find to be preserved, and which eventually reached the National Museum, was a small square plaque, found on the skeleton's chest.

Religious bronzes of this type were made at Limoges in France in the 13th century, and it is probable the Benbecula plaque originated there. Large numbers were manufactured for use in churches throughout Europe, but the quality of the art seems to have suffered in order to produce larger quantities.

David Caldwell researched all of these details for the National Museum and published them in 1980. He reported that only one other enamelled bronze from Limoges had ever been found in Scotland - a figure of Christ, 17 cm tall, found in 1883 in the churchyard of Ceres, Fife; this is also now in the Museum.

A great deal remains in the realms of speculation.

- Was the plaque already old by the time that it reached Borve?
- By what route did it travel from Limoges to Benbecula?
- Did a chief of Clan Ranald purchase it, or acquire it in a raid, or receive it as a gift?
- Was it ever used on a wooden cross in Teampull Bhuirgh?
- Had it already been adapted as part of a priest's vestments?
- Who was the individual prestigious enough to have the plaque buried with him?

CHAPTER 31

IRON AGE AND VIKING
HOMES AT DRIMORE

More fascinating questions arise from excavations at Drimore.

- Can a folk memory last for 15,000 generations or more ?
- Was an ancestor of the Highland Terrier living on an Iron Age farm?
- Did the design of the Hebridean Blackhouse originate with the Vikings?

Several digs were carried out in 1956 prior to development of the South Uist Rocket Range, with nothing left visible on site. One of the archaeologists commented that '... *after excavation, all walling which had been exposed was levelled to avoid accidents to grazing cattle. Vegetation and blowing sand took over, and the site can now be located only with difficulty.*'

The 'Big Smiddy'

An oval hillock near Drimore, known to locals as A' Cheardach Mhòr (the Big Smiddy – smithy, blacksmith's), was situated about three hundred yards from the shore and stood about six feet six inches above the general level of the flat grazing land around it. Stones had been taken from it as they were exposed by erosion, while burrowing rabbits sometimes disturbed fragments of pottery and bone.

Alison Young and K M Richardson directed an excavation there during May and June 1956. The site had been 'sealed' by blown sand, resulting in a remarkable degree of preservation. Together with the finding of

123

several almost complete cooking pots, this may indicate that the site was abandoned in a sudden emergency.

The site proved to be a fairly well-preserved Iron Age wheelhouse, a term which derives from the 'rim-and-spokes' appearance of the ground plan. Nineteen feet in diameter, the interior of the circular house was divided by piers that extended radially towards a central hearth. Three of these piers still stood four feet tall above floor level.

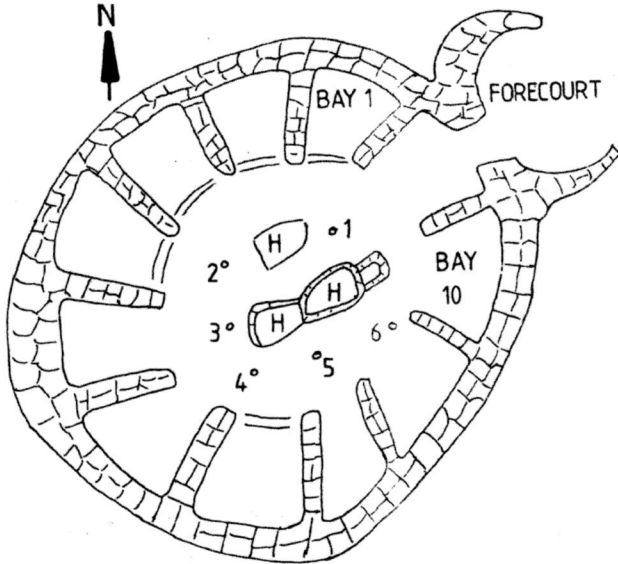

Sketch plan of the Iron Age wheelhouse
excavated at A' Cheardach Mhòr, Drimore.

The bays between the piers of the wheelhouse (the spokes
of the 'wheel') were numbered anti-clockwise from 1 to 10.
'H' marks hearths at the centre of the house.

Numbers 1 to 6 represent holes for wooden posts which supported
the roof. 1 and 5 were formed from perforated whale vertebrae, each
about a foot in diameter. The other four holes were conventionally
dug in the floor, one with a smaller spade-shaped piece of whalebone
used as a wedge. Redrawn from Young and Richardson, 1959.

When occupied, the separate bays of the wheelhouse would have allowed a certain amount of personal privacy, or provided areas for different occupations, or both, while all areas received warmth from a central hearth. No roofing material was found in the excavation, but it is often assumed that wheelhouses had conical roofs of timber and thatch.

Bones of domestic stock found at the site included sheep and oxen, with some pig and horse; while shells of oyster, mussel, whelk and razor were found throughout the soil levels. There was a definite heap of razor shells at one point, and areas of closely-packed limpet shells.

The excavators speculated that a trimmed shoulder-blade might have been a scoop for shellfish; while two small whale vertebrae, hollowed out to form rough cups, may have been used as oil-lamps.

Bones from two dogs were also discovered, one of them probably a hunting dog of similar size to a modern retriever. The remains of the other dog were of considerable interest, as they belonged to a much smaller animal. A D Clark, in his report on the bones within Young and Richardson's 1959 paper, wrote that they were the bones of a *small working terrier comparable with, and surely ancestral to, the ancient broken-haired Highland Terrier from which have descended the Skye, Cairn and Aberdeen Terriers'.*

A sequence of pottery types suggests that the wheelhouse was occupied over a long period of time. In their report, the authors noted the similarity of the finds to those at comparable levels at Jarlshof, Shetland. They doubted, however, that seamanship at the time would have been good enough to forge a direct link between the two communities. Nowadays, archaeologists are more prepared to accept a marine connection between the Hebrides and Shetland during the Iron Age, or even earlier. (See Patrick Ashmore's comments in chapter 43.)

One fragment of pot had the cast of a sea-worm on it. Was this picked up on the shore by an inhabitant and taken back to the house? A collection of beach pebbles seemed to have been deliberately gathered. Both could be interpreted as evidence for childish curiosity and games … the collections of razor shells and limpets, as well? (My speculation, not the dig directors'.)

The more conventional archaeologist's explanation for the sea-worm-pot is that the sea inundated the house, leading to its abandonment. As so often happens, an archaeological story ends with questions that may be unanswerable.

The 'Little Smiddy'

In 1956 Horace Fairhurst excavated a low hillock on Drimore machair known as A' Cheardach Bheag, the Little Smiddy. Like the Big Smiddy, this site also proved to be a wheelhouse, but of a rather strange type. During its long period of use the wheelhouse was adapted to changing conditions.

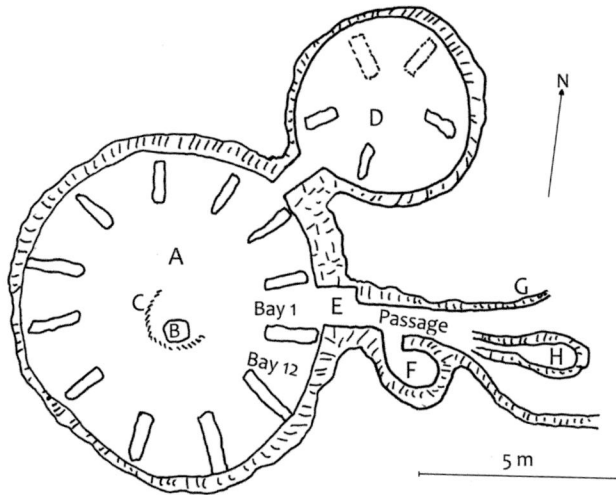

Sketch-plan of the Little Smiddy. Features A – H are explained below.
Redrawn from Fairhurst, 1971.

The main wheelhouse (A) had a nineteen-foot internal diameter. It seemed that, at first, the only feature outside the main house was a short entrance porch or forecourt (E). The house was built with its floor well below the general level of the machair. Gradually sand encroached on the building.

Further stone walling was added to the porch in stages, making it into a passage which grew longer and longer (G). Part of the main house was ruined by the sand, and this is probably when the smaller wheelhouse (D) was added, with a short passage, to provide more living space.

The central hearth consisted of a flat stone slab (B), cracked into several pieces. The oddest feature of the whole site was a 'kerb' about two-and-a-half feet from this hearth, an arc of twenty bones (C). Each bone was the left or right half of a *red deer's lower jaw*! The upper surface of each jaw, with the teeth, was pushed firmly into the ground and overlapped with the next bone. They were not burnt or even scorched by the fire. In his report, the excavator called this peculiar feature a *'bizarre assemblage... vaguely gruesome... ritual was obviously involved ...'*, but left any further speculation to the imaginations of his readers. As do I!

The furnace (H) went out of use before it was enclosed by the passage. Built with flat rounded slabs brought from the bench, it was the shape of an upturned boat measuring twelve-and-a-half feet by four-and-a-half feet, with a four-foot long flue. No mortar or clay was used in its construction.

The furnace was clearly not a pottery kiln, nor was it of the right type for use as a corn-drying kiln. Lumps of vitrified clay suggests that it reached a high temperature. This would have required a forced draught, so the flue may have contained a large pair of bellows. As an Iron Age structure, was the furnace used for smelting iron from iron ore? ... unlikely, as no slag, the inevitable waste from smelting, was found.

The one metal object excavated from the whole site was an iron ploughshare, of a suitable shape for use on the machair. This and other evidence suggested that the furnace was a forge used by a blacksmith. Can the Gaelic name A' Cheardach Bheag – Little Smiddy – really be a folk tradition passed down through thousands of generations, even through language changes of the inhabitants?

Many years after Fairhurst's excavation, part of a brooch of copper alloy with gilding was found on the site. Probably from the Norse period, it clearly dated from centuries after the wheelhouse was last occupied.

A Viking 'Blackhouse'

About three hundred metres from the shore at Drimore, Alastair MacLaren and his team excavated a structure with thick walls, constructed of double dry-stone walling, with a fill of earth or turf. The end walls were curved, there was a central hearth and there was a doorway about a third of the way along one long wall.

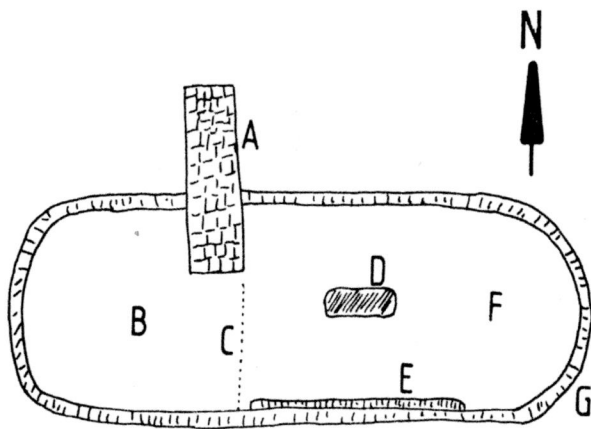

Sketch plan of the Viking house excavated at Drimore.
Redrawn from MacLaren, 1971.

A - Paved ramp up to and through entrance door
B - Western third of the house, with few finds - livestock?
C - Functional division between areas B and F (no trace of dividing wall found)
D - Hearth
E - Stone bench along internal wall
F - Eastern two-thirds of house, many finds, hearth and bench — domestic?
G - Rounded end wall

Most of the archaeologists' finds came from the two-thirds of the house floor to the left of the entrance, the other third being almost free of finds. This suggested to the excavator that there was a 'functional division' between the two sections of the building, although no trace of an internal wall was found. But it is an important archaeological principle that the lack of evidence for some feature must never be taken as proof that the feature itself was missing - *'the absence of evidence is not evidence of absence'*.

However, no-one familiar with the traditional Hebridean blackhouse will be surprised by the conclusion drawn by the dig directors. The larger section was a domestic area, including a hearth and a wall-bench — while the smaller area was occupied by livestock. What may surprise some people is that this basic 'blackhouse design' was in use as early the 9th century AD.

The finds around the hearth area suggest a way of life based on pastoral farming, with some hunting and gathering. Seven types of shellfish were eaten in some quantity — cockles, limpets, oysters, mussels, scallops, whelks and winkles. A few cod bones were found, but no fishing gear, so it seems unlikely that fishing was important. Red deer bones and antlers suggested some hunting.

Bones of domestic creatures included ox, sheep, pig, horse and dog. In addition, there were the bones of greater black-backed gull, razorbill and duck — all of which were no doubt caught and eaten.

Surprisingly little pottery was found; domestic vessels and spindle whorls were made from steatite. This is a soft stone that must have been imported from Shetland or Norway by the Viking settlers. While the whorls indicate that spinning was undertaken in the house, there were no loom-weights or combs, so it is unlikely that the inhabitants were also weavers.

No weapons were found, consistent with a settled farming community at peace with its neighbours. A small bone gaming piece was found. A tiny fragment of silver plate was decorated with ring and dot motifs, but unfortunately was much too small for its purpose to be determined.

Several pieces of whalebone were found in the house, the most interesting of which was a 'cleaver', a tool used in the preparation of leather. Similar tools had never before been found in Scotland, and they were not common even in Norway.

The Drimore house was probably the nucleus of a small farmstead of the late 9th or early 10th century AD, a largely self-sufficient unit. As at the Big Smiddy, the finds were comparable with those at Jarlshof in Shetland. No-one would doubt seaborne connections at the time of the far-flung 'Viking empire'.

Drimore 1956

Other digs took place at Drimore in 1956, prior to the development of the Rocket Range, but only those by Fairhurst, by MacLaren and by Young and Richardson appear to have been published in detail.

CHAPTER 32

THE UNDERGROUND HOUSE ON BARRA

On a rocky hillock in moorland, inland from Allasdale on Barra, is the site known as Tigh Talamhanta (the underground house). A wheelhouse and its surroundings were excavated by Lindsay Scott and by Alison Young between 1950 and 1953, over a decade before Young's Drimore excavations.

Euan MacKie, writing in 2007, compared the wheelhouse here with the 'Big Smiddy' at Drimore about 30 miles to the north. He commented that Tigh Talamhanta, being on the moors with no encroaching sand, provides a better idea of the layout of an Iron Age farmstead than does any site in the machair. At Drimore, while accumulated sand had protected the interior of the wheelhouse, sand in the surroundings had hidden possible associated buildings.

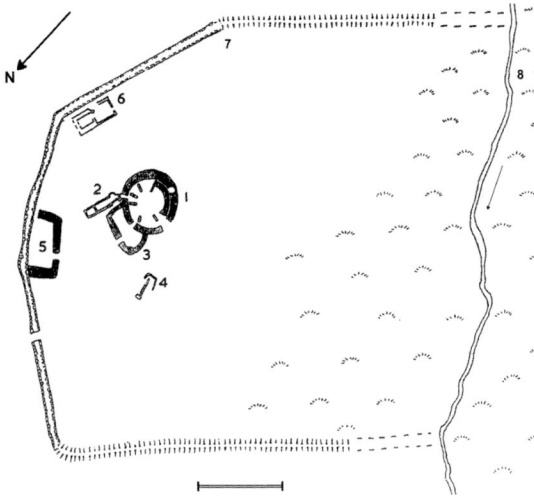

Plan of the Talamhanta farmstead. Scale of 50 feet. Features 1 - 8 are explained below. Adapted from Young, 1958.

The wheelhouse (1 on plan) of Talamhanta was 36 feet in diameter, with seven of nine internal piers surviving. A black deposit in the central area was thought to be the remains of a collapsed roof. The main doorway opened out to a space defined by a wall (7), partly of stone, partly turf. A fast-flowing stream (8) formed part of the boundary. With an area of over 640 square yards, it was considered to be a farmyard, with rough rock-cut steps leading down the hill. Structure 4 was considered an 'outside working area'.

A second exit led into a rectangular building with a paved floor (3), probably a lean-to, described as a 'kiln house'. It had an outside vent suggesting that it might have been used for corn drying. At a third gap in the wall, there were two steps down into a souterrain (2). This was a low passage capped with lintels, probably used as a storage area. A rock-cut drain led downwards from it.

A rectangular building (5) was set against the farmyard wall to the north of, and down a slope from, the house. The two sections were interpreted as a barn and a byre, though each had a hearth. A slab of stone at the barn entrance had an obvious circular depression, the pivot for a door. A building (6) to the west of the wheelhouse was a later addition to the site.

There were many potsherds but very few finds of bone. A few iron finds included a ring large enough to tether an animal, two fragments of knives, a strap-end and a pin shaft. Other artefacts included an unusual type of bronze brooch with possible links to Gaul; fragments of mounds for bronze working; bits of glass beads; flint flakes and a quartz scraper.

The site was considered the homestead with outbuildings and yard of a small self-sufficient farming community. The brooch and the beads suggested contacts with the outside world.

CHAPTER 33

FARMING, HUNTING AND FISHING AT NORTHTON

Derek Simpson of Leicester University was the author of numerous archaeological books and director of many excavations. At the conference on Western Isles archaeology held in Edinburgh in 1983, he gave a lecture on his work in 1966 and 1967 at Northton, South Harris. He explained that his dig had been situated on machair at the foot of Chaipaval, the conical hill that dominates the scenery of the south-west corner of Harris.

Much of the site must have been destroyed by coastal erosion before Simpson's team started work; however, important evidence remained. The site had six occupation levels, separated by layers of windblown sand. The two lowest levels were Neolithic, the next two were of the Beaker period (Chalcolithic to Early Bronze Age), while the upper two were of Iron Age and historic date. Most of the material excavated consisted of middens – ancient refuse piles – the collections of food debris, broken tools and pottery, etc., which archaeologists find so fascinating and informative.

TOE
HEAD

CHAIPAVAL

SOUTH HARRIS

RUBH AN
TEAMPULL

DIG
SITE

NORTHTON

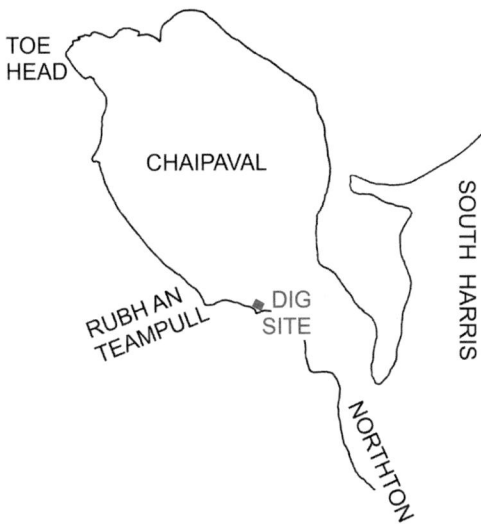

The position of Derek Simpson's
1966-67 excavations at Northton.

Evidence from Snail Shells

At peaty sites pollen is well preserved and provides evidence for the ancient environment. Northton, a sandy site, contained no preserved pollen, so attempts to reconstruct the local environment in the past had to use alternative evidence – the shells of land snails that had been preserved in each sandy layer.

Once the numerous species had been identified, they were grouped into those nowadays normally found in open countryside, and those which generally prefer the shade of woodland. The proportions in each layer were used to decide whether or not the area was wooded at the time. However, not all archaeologists and biologists have accepted the use of this method, as its conclusions conflict with pollen evidence from elsewhere on the island. 'Woodland snails' might have lived in tall grassland in a mild damp climate.

Taking the snail evidence at face value suggested that woodland was cleared in Neolithic time, with the land remaining treeless for around a thousand years. Among mammal bones, those of sheep predominated. Bone and snail evidence together implied a pastoral way of life in relatively open countryside.

Beaker Period

The evidence collected from the Beaker levels is fascinating. The presence of woodland, as suggested by snail species, is supported by evidence from antlers. Remains of red deer antlers uncovered in the dig were from really large stags, typical of deer feeding in woodland rather than on moorland.

So we can imagine the Beaker period inhabitants of Harris hunting deer in a wooded countryside, butchering them for food, and making leather from the skins. Finds of bone points, bone spatulas and rubbing stones could all have been used in leather-working. As the Minch is too wide for red deer to swim, Simpson suggested that a stock of deer may have been transported to Harris by early settlers in their boats.

Fine layers of windblown sand were found between layers of Beaker period midden, which might suggest seasonal occupation, sand sometimes engulfing the site while the inhabitants were away. Evidence from the study of bird bones seemed to contradict this; both the great auk and the fieldfare appear to have formed part of the diet. As the now-extinct great auk was a summer visitor and the fieldfare is a winter visitor, people must have been living at the site at both times of year. A layer of sand could have resulted from a single bad storm.

Beaker period communities are normally thought of as farming settlements ... but perhaps not at Northton. The middens contained no evidence of cereal production – no preserved grains, no quern stones, no impressions of grains on pottery. Despite the principle that 'absence of evidence is not evidence of absence', it does seem very likely that they were not growing cereals.

Bones of red deer outnumbered those of sheep and other domestic species. There were also bones of marine mammals and of fish, including wrasse, conger eel and cod. Limpet shells were joined by those of crabs, lobsters and sea urchins. The clear implication is that the Beaker period community at Northton was living mainly by hunting and fishing.

Tools such as arrowheads and scrapers were made from various stones. Flint could have been collected only as beach pebbles. Quartz came from an obvious outcrop on the hill above the site. Serpentine is found within two miles. Tools of a fourth material were also found, possibly mylonite (see chapter 47). Pumice, used as an abrasive cleaner, is a volcanic stone. It is so light that it floats; pieces could have drifted from Iceland to be found washed up on the shore at Northton.

A tiny scrap of bronze found in the upper Beaker level is the only evidence for metal-working at the site. It is probably just a fragment that had splashed out of a mould during the casting process. It is impossible to say whether it was produced from imported metal ores — or whether a used metal tool was being melted down for re-casting.

In the lower (older) of the two Beaker levels, two built structures were distinguished. They could be called houses, but may have been little more than rough shelters against the wind. The oval shape of the more complete structure led to the suggestion that it might have been roofed by an upturned boat.

The collection of domestic pottery from the Beaker layers was, at that time, the largest from any Scottish site. Sherds from that period, and from the Neolithic layers, were examined microscopically for mineral content, which proved identical to that of the natural boulder clay of the area. Thus it was conclusively – and unsurprisingly – proved that local clay was used in the production of pottery. The style of completed Neolithic pots showed close links with those found at Eilean an Tighe in North Uist.

Evidence from Sea Shells

Marine shells gave clues to changing sea levels. In the Neolithic, the most numerous shells were of bivalves such as cockles, suggesting extensive tidal sand-flats and thus a relatively low sea level. In the Beaker levels, limpets were present in the greatest numbers. As limpets live on rocky shores, this suggests a higher sea level.

As the title of the Conference was 'Neolithic and Bronze Age Settlement in the Western Isles', Derek's talk made little reference to the Iron Age levels, except for the evidence from mollusc shells. Of land shells, the most numerous were of open-land species, suggesting that the woodland was cleared – indeed the landscape has remained treeless up to the present day. Of marine shells, bivalves were most numerous, suggesting that sea level was lower than in the Bronze Age.

Turf-covered enclosures on the top of the dune probably related to a later period. The area remained inhabited for centuries; on the next headland to the west, Rubh an Teampull, are the ruins of a small late medieval chapel, itself based on the footings of an Iron Age broch.

The inhabitants of the Northton site, through changes of culture, adapted their way of life to available resources over the centuries. Whether most of their food came from farming or from hunting and fishing, they were able to obtain or to make the articles necessary for their life-style.

A Mesolithic Layer

Further small scale excavations were undertaken by Dr Mike Church at the site in 2001. From a layer with evidence of human occupation, hazel-nut shells were radiocarbon dated to the Mesolithic period, over 9000 years before the present day, one of the earliest known dates for human occupation in the Western Isles.

CHAPTER 34

A FAIRY KNOLL AND
PLOUGH MARKS AT ROSINISH

A name such as Sithean Rosinish is a clue to an archaeologist, as the Gaelic place-name element 'Sithean', meaning fairy knoll, often proves to be an indication of ancient occupation. The name may result from a folk memory of earlier cultures, or from local structures seeming alien in origin. Late in the eighteenth century, there was a Benbecula tradition of leaving milk libations for the supposed inhabitants of Sithean Rosinish.

Bronze Age Burial

Following erosion of the Sithean hillock, Peter Morrison and Neil Macaskill from the nearby island of Grimsay found the top of a stone dome. They opened the dome and removed most of the contents — including human bones. The two amateur excavators reported the matter to Iain Crawford, well-known for his long-running dig on North Uist. With the support of the National Museum, and helped by a conveniently excellent ten-day spell of weather in August 1964, Crawford undertook a systematic examination of the area.

The main structure was a beehive-shaped stone tomb about five feet across. It must have been hidden below an earth mound for almost 4,000 years yet it had remained 'sand-tight', the cavity completely unsilted. It had contained the fragmentary remains of three skeletons – a male aged about 40 and two females of around 20.

Beyond the dome, but not concentric with it, a ring of slabs ten feet in diameter had been placed. Perhaps it was a later construction – sometime after the burial dome had been built, it may have been almost hidden by blown sand. To ensure that the position of the dome was not lost, the circle may have been created as a marker. There were two other small stone chambers nearby, but no further burials.

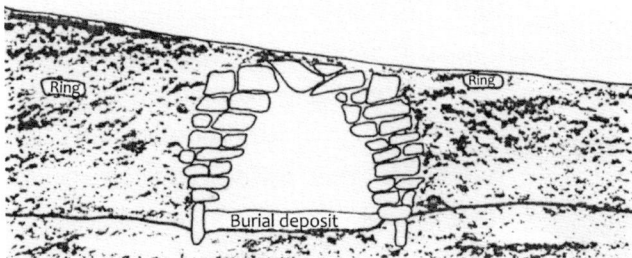

A vertical section showing the shape of the Rosinish burial dome and two stones of the later ring. Redrawn from Crawford, 1977.

137

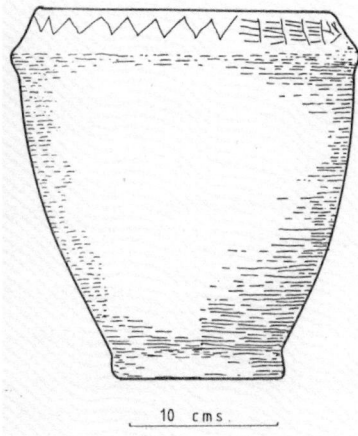

A reconstruction drawing of a pot found with the Rosinish burials. Like two others, the pot had been found in fragments. Redrawn from Crawford, 1977.

Crawford struggled to find any direct parallels in the archaeological literature, either for the domed tomb or for the decorated pottery. The people at Rosinish appeared to have 'invented' their own local burial structure and to have adapted their pottery designs from traditional Beaker period styles.

Plough Marks

Crawford found that there were occupation deposits in many of the sand levels of his excavation. This resulted in more extensive work around Sithean Rosinish in 1975, '76 and '77, led by Ian Shepherd and Alexandra Shepherd (then Tuckwell). When the sand surface in a sample square was carefully scraped with a trowel, slightly darker lines appeared – plough marks. Several running parallel to each other indicated the general direction of ploughing.

Plough marks are clear evidence for cultivation of crops. The development of crop growing was one of mankind's most significant inventions. To archaeologists, it marks the great divide between the semi-nomadic hunters of the Mesolithic on the one hand, and the settled agriculturalists of the Neolithic on the other. Excavators are always on the lookout for evidence that crops were grown.

The best indication that a society grew crops is finding preserved cereal

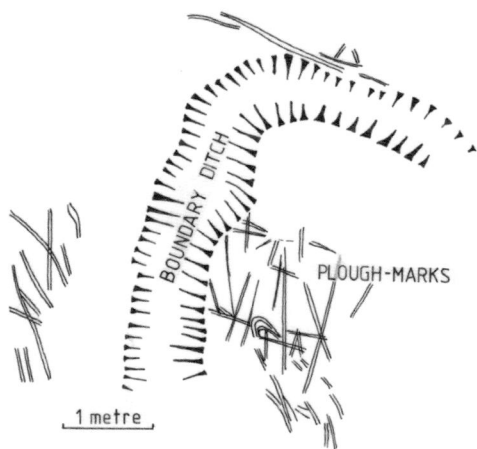

The excavators found a curved ditch about 4 metres long and 4.5 metres wide. This was assumed to have been part of a field boundary, with separate sets of plough-marks on each side. Redrawn from Shepherd and Tuckwell, 1979.

grains. At Rosinish, soil samples were laboriously sieved, resulting in the find of 170 individual grains, later identified in the laboratory. Almost all were of barley, well known from Beaker period sites — perhaps they grew it to make beer to fill their Beakers! However, unusually for this latitude, five grains were of emmer, a primitive type of wheat. It is unlikely that wheat was a very successful crop in the climatic conditions of Benbecula.

Quern-stones are another form of evidence for cultivation. While it is possible to make a kind of flour by grinding up the seeds of wild grasses, the existence of querns is generally taken to indicate a cereal-growing community.

Additionally, metal sickles are commonly found in Bronze Age and Iron Age sites, evidence for the harvesting of cereals, but what type of sickle was used in the Neolithic? I am reminded of a seven-inch-long flint sickle, which I was able to borrow from Ipswich Museum in the early 1970s when setting up a village history exhibition. Looking at the sharp edge of the blade with a magnifying glass, I could see a lustre created by cutting the stems of corn.

In the west of Scotland, it would be very unusual to find such a tool, as supplies of large flint nodules are uncommon. However, a sickle might have been made by mounting a series of small flakes of flint or quartz along a wooden or bone support, rather like the teeth of a saw.

139

Returning to the Rosinish plough-marks – by carefully scraping out the darker soil, the shape of the tool used was revealed. The V-shaped marks had one side vertical and the other curved, suggesting that a wooden 'crook ard' was probably used. This was a kind of light plough; a similar one found at Hvorslev in Denmark was dated to around 1825 BC, while one from Gwithian in Cornwall appears to have had a stone tip to the wooden blade of the ard. The plough would probably have been supported by one man and pulled along by another man, rather than by a horse or ox.

Reading Shepherd and Tuckwell's 1979 paper, I learned something of the history of the Rosinish fields. On at least two occasions, north-westerly winds eroded the ploughed area or submerged it in blown sand. Midden material, including potsherds and limpet shells, was deposited on the sand-blow to stabilise it, and ploughing recommenced on the new surface. Limpets from the earliest midden layer were dated to around 2385 BC.

Perhaps anyone cultivating a patch of land, large or small, in the present day might give a thought to the people of Rosinish, who were trying to maintain cultivation around 4400 years ago, despite blown sand invading their lands.

CHAPTER 35

DUN CARLOWAY BROCH

Dun Carloway is often the next stop for tourists after the Callanish Stones, some visitors perhaps unaware that the broch was built when the Stones were already thousands of years old. By tradition, it was *built by the giant Darg Mac Nu-Aran*' in the fourth century AD! In fact, it was probably built by an Iron Age society around 200 BC, one of over

Dun Carloway Broch is the second-best preserved of Scotland's brochs, after Mousa in Shetland. Its walls rise 30 feet at their highest remaining part and may have been over 40 feet high originally.

five hundred brochs unique to the north and west of Scotland. They are drystone towers, the tallest manmade structures of prehistoric Britain. Sadly most remaining today are ruinous, simply piles of stone.

Construction and Use

As tall structures, often built on already high ground, brochs were vulnerable to Atlantic gales. However, they were immensely strong, despite being built without the use of mortar. Strength came from their double construction, with cavities between upright inner walls and inward-sloping outer walls. Slabs of stone bonded the inner and outer walls, some of them forming stairs or galleries.

Howard Atkinson, writing in *Popular Archaeology* in 1983, believed that there were internal lean-to structures around the inside wall, leaving an open central area, with arrangements for collecting rainfall. It is now thought more likely that ledges on the inner walls, known as scarcements, supported one or more complete wooden floors, and that the high wall-tops were capped by a conical thatched roof. The area below the lowest floor might have accommodated only sheep or other livestock.

With high walls and a single entrance, protected by a supposed 'guard cell' (chamber D on the plan on page 144), it seems obvious to visitors that brochs were intended for defence from invaders. The Gaelic word *'dùn'* is generally applied to a castle or other defensive structure. However, it is very rare to find weapons in broch excavations. Also, brochs do not have wells, essential for surviving a siege. On the contrary, there is more often evidence of a peaceful way of life – such as quern stones and tools for weaving or sewing.

It has been suggested that brochs were the equivalent of 'stately homes' and this may well be true of the larger brochs. Their dominant size and position would have demonstrated the prestige of important people (chieftains ?) living there. The amount of wood needed for internal floors and roof beams would have been conspicuous consumption in a treeless landscape. Smaller brochs may have been more equivalent to farmhouses. I'm reminded of the very wide variety and differing sizes of buildings designated as 'chateaux' in France.

Origin of the Design

There has been much speculation about where the idea of building brochs originated; did they spread south from Orkney or north from Skye? Seumas Caulfield, a Dublin archaeologist, published a paper in 1980 attempting to answer this question. He analysed published excavation reports and other records of brochs, some from as far back as 1851, concentrating on finds of quern stones.

In Iron Age times, as the name suggests, iron became generally used, at least for weapons. But for ordinary families, a more significant change was an improvement in the method used to grind grain. The traditional saddle quern was quite inefficient. A rounded stone was dragged back and forth over grain placed in the central depression of a large flat stone. In the 'new' rotary quern, an upper circular millstone was rotated by hand on a lower stationary millstone, also circular, grinding the grain between them. The same principle was later applied in larger water-driven mills.

Rotary querns were a vast improvement on saddle querns. Just as the washboard and tub were replaced by the washing machine in the 20th century, so prehistoric 'housewives' must have been pleased to replace their saddle querns once the rotary type was available. In neither case would anyone wish to return to the older technology!

Thus the rotary quern must have spread gradually through Scotland. Caulfield found records of *both* types of quern in brochs on the northern mainland and in Orkney. However, brochs on the west coast and in the Hebrides mostly had only rotary querns. He concluded that the design of brochs originated in the north, spreading southwards around the west coast.

There have been many other studies since on the origin of brochs, but this forty-year-old study appealed to me, perhaps because, like some of our research at Callanish, a new theory had been produced just by studying old documents.

Excavation

The only excavation in Dun Carloway itself, in 1972, was confined to one small chamber. Christopher Tabraham and Colin Bowman found three hearths with peat ash, a clay-lined pit, hundreds of fragments of pottery, one broken quern-stone, and some limpet shells. They believed that the hearths were intended for the firing of pots; that this had been a potter's workshop during a secondary occupation of the site between AD 400 and 700.

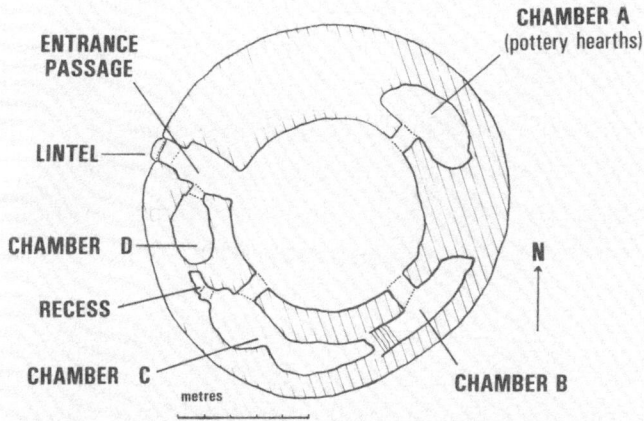

I prepared this plan in 1980 and used it in our
four-page publication, *A Mini-guide to Dun Carloway
Broch*. It was the first available visitor information,
apart from an on-site panel. Today, the Dun has
a small stone-built Visitor Centre.

Later Occupation

Some brochs no doubt proved useful in defence on occasion, even centuries after their Iron Age occupation. According to a story from the seventeenth century, Dun Carloway was a stronghold for members of the Morison clan of Ness, during their long-standing feud with the Macaulays of Uig. Donald Cam Macaulay reputedly ended a siege by climbing the outer wall of the dun, using two dirks as climbing irons, smothering the Morisons by throwing burning heather into the central area.

As late as the 1870 s *'there still was a respectable looking family living in the ground flat of the broch'*.

144

PART 5

Finds and Excavations, 1975–1984

———

All of the discoveries detailed in this section are ones in which I had some form of personal involvement, sometimes featuring them in my *Stornoway Gazette* columns.

CHAPTER 36

BRONZE AGE BURIAL
AT KNEEP

By the summer of 1976, we were in contact with Patrick Ashmore about our documentary research on the Callanish Stones. Visiting the island, he introduced us to Joanna Close-Brooks of the National Museum, who was looking for volunteer helpers to excavate a cairn in the west of Lewis. It was the school holidays and we were free to help, within family constraints.

The cairn was near the little settlement of Kneep, on a headland overlooking the superb beach of Traigh na Berie. We worked with Joanna's team during their two weeks at the site. Often I was the 'labourer', moving barrow-loads of sand, only occasionally joining Margaret and the others on our knees doing careful work with trowels. It was our first introduction to 'dirt archaeology' … and to the often convivial evenings after a day on site! Joanna was by now inured to the jokes that her initials, JCB, were very appropriate for an 'excavator'. A second season in 1978 was needed to complete the excavation, plough marks of the Early Bronze Age being found at the lowest level.

Due to erosion, upper stones of the cairn had been visible for some years. The dig proved that there had been three levels, each with a burial. After the removal of stones of the upper cairn, a lower, earlier, cairn was exposed, its edge stones forming a very obvious, if unusual, D-shape. It

Excavation of the Kneep cairn in progress. The three upright slabs are those remaining of the rectangular cist in the centre of the D-shaped cairn. Before this photograph was taken, two capstones had been put to one side.

measured about six by seven metres and had a much smaller rectangular cist at its centre.

When, in a later period, a deeper circular cist was cut into the rectangular one, two uprights were removed, and human bones thrown aside. Within the cist was a plain urn resting on a flat floor slab. It had been placed upside-down, so it is likely that funerary material was initially kept in place by a fabric covering. When reported, it was the only known cremation – in an urn – from the Western Isles. Black residue stuck to the inside of the vessel was radiocarbon dated to approximately 1450 BC.

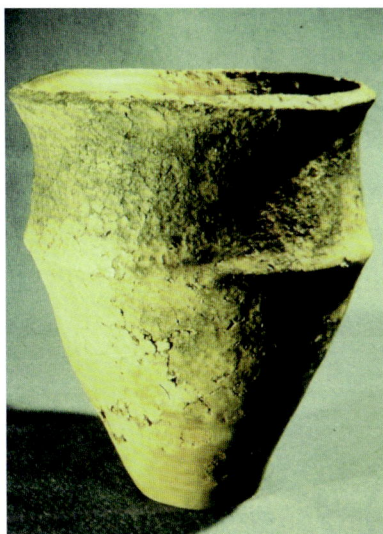

This unusually plain funerary urn, here seen restored after conservation, was found in the circular cist. Image © National Museums Scotland

A mysterious substance called cramp, a vitreous slag, was found here as at other island sites. It was thought to have been formed by a reaction between bone and seaweed, perhaps also shell sand, in the heat of a pyre. Reading Joanna's full report in a 1995 journal, I was surprised to find this sentence – *An attempt by Gerald Ponting to produce cramp by heating animal bones and seaweed to a high temperature in the laboratories of the Nicolson Institute, Stornoway, produced only awful smells in the school corridors.'* Experimental archaeology!

Research in Orkney, published in 2007, suggested that cramp was produced when seaweed was used as fuel for a pyre, resulting in vitrification of attached sand particles.

CHAPTER 37

RESCUE EXCAVATION AT EOROPIE

In September 1977, contractors were preparing a site at Eoropie for a new house to be built for a returning native. They had found bones and what they took to be a stone-built underground tunnel. Members of the Ness Archaeological Club took an interest, and one of their members phoned and asked us to take a look at the site.

We felt that it was some form of ancient dwelling, so we contacted two of the official bodies in Edinburgh. Neither was able to send a representative, so they suggested that we should undertake a rescue excavation ourselves and record any structures found. Thus, for a couple of damp weekends, assisted by members of the Ness club, we laboured in a hole in the ground, no doubt with none of the Health and Safety considerations that would be observed today.

The layer nearest the present ground level appeared to be a midden, with large quantities of animal bones including those of cow, sheep, deer and pig, as well as limpet shells. This immediately suggested a farming community which also hunted and used marine resources. One piece of bone had been sharpened to form a pin. Large beach stones with one end damaged had been used as hammer stones.

Numerous shattered pebbles ('potboilers') in the midden provided evidence for a prehistoric method of cooking. Beach pebbles, of about tennis-ball size, were heated in the fire and then dropped into a clay pot of water, or probably stew. The pebbles often cracked in the process.

Below the midden layer was a complex of structures built as dry-stone walls. There was a paved area and an under-floor 'drain' covered by lintel-like slabs, which led to a stone-lined pit. Nearby was a rough mound of flattened stones. We took photographs and prepared plans as the structures were uncovered; and in due course back-filled the site before the contractors returned. We published a summary of our findings in *'Discovery and Excavation in Scotland'* 1977.

Melia Hedges, an archaeological researcher from Edinburgh University, was able to visit Lewis and examine the site; she provisionally dated some of the pottery to the early Iron Age. Local knowledge that stone structures had been found, when digging foundations on previous occasions, suggested that there might have been an extensive Iron Age settlement in the area. Ms Hedges took samples away with her for analysis – sadly, I have found no record of her results.

An article about the discovery in the *Stornoway Gazette* included a long quotation from the Procurator Fiscal, Colin Scott Mackenzie. He joked that the discovery was *'alleged to be a secret tunnel from the original Stone Age bothan at Eoropie'*. But his main concern was to remind the public that any *'ancient buried objects, including bones, artefacts, buildings, teeth'* constitute Treasure Trove under Scottish law and should be reported to an official grandly known as the Queen's and Lord Treasurer's Remembrancer* – or locally to the Fiscal.

An Unusual Thank-You Gift

One evening we gave a presentation of our findings to an audience in Ness. When thanking us, one of our new friends offered some form of reward. My reply was – *'please get me a guga'*. Each year a group from

---

* Today, the Q&LTR is of course the *King's* and Lord Treasurer's Remembrancer. It is worth noting that while Treasure Trove in Scotland includes ancient objects of any material, in England it covers only precious objects of gold and silver,.

Ness spends two weeks on the remote island of Sula Sgeir, harvesting large numbers of gannet chicks – gugas – which are considered delicacies by many locals. It is a centuries-old tradition, which continues under licence despite the Protection of Birds Act. As an 'incomer' I would have had no chance to obtain one and discover the flavour of such a unique local dish.

A few weeks later one of my pupils at the Nicolson, a lad from Ness, presented me with a smelly plastic bag. On unwrapping the guga at home, it looked a bit like a spatchcocked chicken, but with a fishy smell. We cooked the bird, a long slow boil, and the four of us sat down to try it, with a plateful of home-grown vegetables … an intense taste, a sort of cross between chicken and fish, and so rich that a small portion was quite sufficient for one meal. At this distance in time, the guga is clearer in my memory than the excavation.

Eoropie Teampull

In the fields, not far from the site of our excavation, stands a tiny isolated church, also known as Teampull Mholuaidh or St Moluag's. Excavation around the outside walls by John Barber in 1977 proved that the building is all of one period, but could not fix a date. Different pieces of circumstantial evidence suggest that it was built either in the 12th-century … or in the 16th-century.

I published 'A Mini Guide to Eoropie Teampull' in 1981. I was amused to record that, when restored from a ruined state in 1911, the church was furnished with antiquities that would *blend in with the old church and help to trick us into a belief that it had never fallen into disuse*

CHAPTER 38

'VIKING PRINCESS' IN THE DUNES AT KNEEP

I regret to admit that, although I lived for nearly ten years on the Isle of Lewis, I never learnt more than a few words and phrases of Gaelic, though I did become familiar with many place-name elements. Initially, I attended an evening class, but the other members already knew more Gaelic than I did – and I have never been good at languages – so I found it quite impossible and abandoned the attempt. Thus I was never able to follow the news on local Gaelic-speaking radio.

But we had an informant, our local postman, who sometimes passed on headlines that he thought would interest us. This was how we learned in July 1979 that the Procurator Fiscal had dug a skull and grave goods out of the sand somewhere in the Uig area. My immediate thought was that the Fiscal should be preventing grave robbing rather than taking part!

We phoned Colin Scott Mackenzie and learned the full story. He had been called by Will Maclean, who had accidentally come across bones that he took to be human, protruding from the sand dunes above Kneep beach. The Fiscal drove to Kneep, expecting to treat this as a criminal investigation. Other people camping nearby were taking an interest in the bones, and there was no possibility of placing a police guard, so Scott Mackenzie took charge of removing the skeleton, helped by Maclean and a local Detective Constable.

Once grave goods started to appear, it became clear that this was an *archaeological* rather than a criminal investigation. It was decided to remove all of the material for safe keeping – no-one involved being aware that there were, at the time, professional archaeologists working elsewhere

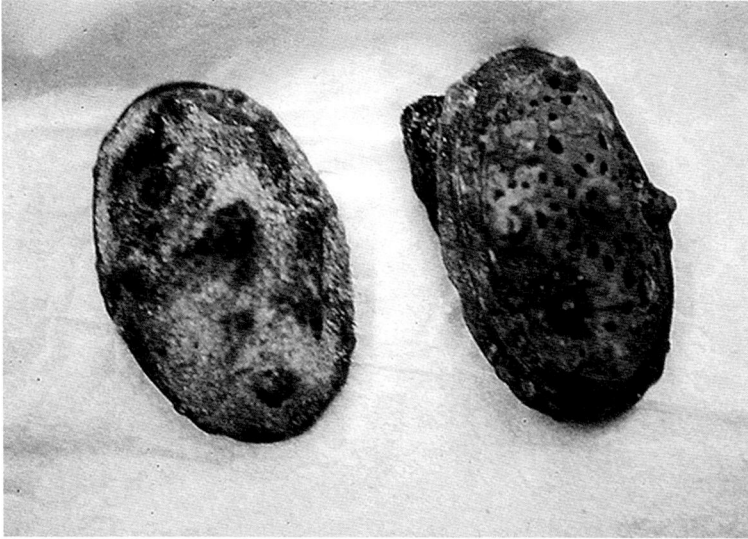

The most spectacular items in the find at Kneep were two tortoise brooches of the early 10th century, probably of Scandinavian manufacture. When first unwrapped from the Procurator Fiscal's ice-cream tubs; they were covered with sand (above) and showed little evidence of ornate decoration. When cleaned in the Edinburgh labs, they proved to be of gilded bronze, braided with silver wire, with variations in ornamentation between the two. Examined in the lab, attached fragments of textile were found to be a known type of Viking fabric. Forty-four glass beads of yellow, blue, silver or gold, most of them segmented, were found loose, but reconstituted into a necklace for the photograph (left). Image © National Museums Scotland on Lewis. So, we felt it our place to contact Trevor Cowie of the National Museum, based with his excavation team at Shawbost School.

We met Trevor and the Fiscal at the latter's home in Stornoway, where the bones and artefacts were stored in large plastic ice-cream tubs. Trevor was very pleased to be given access to the finds, but understandably distressed that he had not been called in at the beginning – amateur excavation destroys the contexts so useful to archaeologists. However, Mr Maclean had made careful notes and taken photographs, which made it possible to reconstruct the disposition of finds and bones, producing diagrams for eventual publication in 'Proceedings of the Society of Antiquaries of Scotland' 1987.

With the team in Shawbost School we watched, fascinated, as the skeleton and the finds were carefully laid out for initial inspection. It was immediately apparent that the burial was of Viking date. As the bones were those of a female, buried with rich grave goods, the find was soon nicknamed the 'Viking Princess'.

In addition to the brooches and beads, other grave goods included a comb made from a deer antler, with incised decoration, its teeth held in place by iron rivets. Two iron needles were enclosed in a needle case made from a hollow bone of a large bird. Other iron objects included a sickle and a rivet, plus a badly eroded iron dagger with fragments of a leather sheath still attached. There were remnants of a belt buckle and strap-end, also a whetstone pendant and a bronze ringed pin.

We later met our friend and bone expert Mary Harman, who had studied the skeleton. She told us that a few of the finger bones were missing. On a day visit to Kneep beach, Margaret took her Breasclete Brownies up to the sand dunes. After I asked the little girls to look around for any small bones on the surface, individuals kept rushing up to me. Usually they had found rabbit bones ... until one Brownie showed me what was obviously a human finger bone. (My original biological education came in handy on occasions!) We sent the bone to Trevor Cowie, and the finder in due course received an official thank-you from the National Museum.

Six more burials were found in Kneep in 1991 and 1994. They were described as belonging to the Viking Age, but isotope analysis showed that none of the individuals was originally from Scandinavia.

CHAPTER 39

THREE STONE AXEHEADS – AND THEN FIVE

Finds of individual stone axeheads are quite common; they may have been lost or abandoned due to wear or breakage. Groups of axeheads are much rarer, often seeming to have been deposited deliberately, for reasons unknown.

When Mr & Mrs A Morrison of Newmarket near Stornoway were cutting peat in 1976, they found three axeheads and a flint near the bottom of the peat bank. The positioning suggested that they might have been buried together, possibly in a bag. This was only the sixth time that a group of axeheads had been recorded in Scotland.

I had the role of photographing them and of being the first to announce them in *DES*. At the National Museum, Joanna Close-Brooks studied them in detail. The three axeheads, each about 11 cm long, were of gneiss, the commonest rock on Lewis, so were probably of local manufacture. It was not possible to tell if they were in mint condition or if they had been used, as they were badly weathered from their centuries in the peat.

Five years later, in August 1981, 12-year-old Iain Mackenzie walked out into the moors from his home in Balallan with his uncle. They intended to fish for trout in Loch Airigh na Ceardaich. On the shore, with the water just rippling over them, Iain noticed 'five old bits of wood' but when he picked one up, he found it to be stone. Each about six

Three stone axeheads found together at Newmarket on Lewis, with a small flint scraper found below their tips. Scale in cm.

inches long, they were too heavy to carry all at once, so they took two home and hid three to collect later.

Probably they had once been buried in peat but water lapping at the shore had uncovered them. Back at home, his family contacted the *Gazette* and a reporter contacted me for comments, some of which were published. Four stone axeheads had been found together in Perthshire in 1902, but this was the first find in Scotland of as many as five axeheads together.

The find proved newsworthy. I received a phone call out of the blue – '*This is Biddy Baxter, the editor of Blue Peter*'. I put her in touch with Iain and he was invited to appear on the programme. Iain and his mother flew to London at BBC expense. The Procurator Fiscal insisted on accompanying the axeheads, as they were Treasure Trove! It was Iain's first visit to the mainland, so he and his mother enjoyed some of the sights of London, and they were given front-row seats at the Savoy theatre.

The Fiscal left the five Ballalan axeheads at the British Museum for transfer back to Scotland for study. The National Museum acquired them under Treasure Trove rules, while Iain eventually received a reward of £150. Talking to a Gazette reporter, he had wondered if he should spend it on fishing tackle, a new bicycle or a snooker table! The newspaper also quoted the museum director – '... *it is actually a very important group of axeheads from the point of view of research that helps to give some idea of, for example, trade movement in the past*'.

And so it proved – while three of the axeheads were probably of local

Iain Mackenzie having his 'fifteen minutes of fame' on *Blue Peter* with presenters Sarah Greene, Simon Groom and Peter Duncan. The programme-makers fitted a handle to one of the axeheads, simply a piece of branch with the bark intact. Watching the show, I immediately commented − *'if Neolithic people could make sophisticated stone axeheads, surely they would not give less attention to the quality of the haft'*. This was soon confirmed on Lewis (see next chapter). Image © BBC Archive

gneiss, surface examination suggested that the other two had been produced at Killin near Loch Tay in Perthshire, the best-known axehead source in Scotland. Over twenty 'axehead factories' are known, scattered throughout the British Isles. Archaeologists now consider the word 'factory' inappropriate for a facility existing four to five thousand years ago, but it took a number of skilled processes to produce a stone axehead.

Each 'factory' was situated where suitable fine-grained stone could be quarried. Basic rough-outs were laboriously shaped into axeheads. An axehead needed grinding, with a succession of abrasives from coarser to finer, to produce a smooth surface and a cutting edge. Many axeheads found today are finely polished, perhaps status symbols rather than tools. This polishing may also have taken many stages.

Geological examination of a tiny sample taken from an axehead can identify the factory from which it came. In this way, it has been proved that there was a considerable trade in axeheads in Neolithic times. Cornish axeheads are found in East Anglia, Lake District axeheads on the Yorkshire coast, while at least one axehead from County Antrim reached Lewis (see next chapter).

Trevor Cowie brought laughter from the audience at a conference on Western Isles archaeology when he remarked – *'I don't think collections of stone axeheads found in the Hebrides were left by axehead factory reps. who had given up in disgust on arriving in a treeless place!'*. He was underlining the fact that finds of axeheads tell us significant things about the past, not least that the landscape included trees that needed to be felled, probably to clear land for crops. There must have been 'travelling salesmen' who transported axeheads around the country.

Early in our studies, we had found a solitary axehead ourselves, among the heather near the single stone of Callanish XI. It was only around seven cm long and badly eroded. It probably remained in Margaret Curtis's collection for decades, till her finds were transferred to museums.

In 1983 I was personally given a stone axehead by a chance acquaintance. In the village of Gravir, Duncan Macleod had helped demolish the ruins of an old stone croft-house built by his great-grandfather. They found the axehead built into one of the walls. I was told that *'the old people had traditions about such axeheads found in the past; building one into*

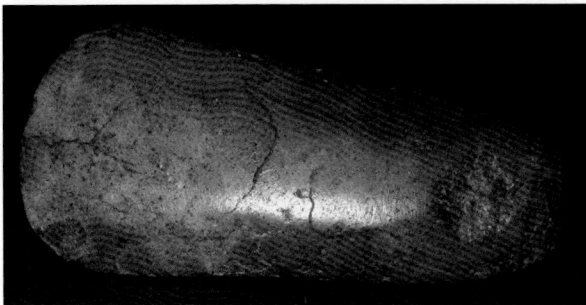

The axehead found in a house ruin at Gravir.

a house wall was supposed to bring good luck'. More prosaically, *'they were found useful as scrapers for cleaning sheep skins'.*

Clearly, no-one knows where Duncan's great-grandfather, or perhaps an earlier generation, had found the axehead. Having been found within a built structure, not in the earth, it has recently been disclaimed by the Treasure Trove Unit. In any case, a single axehead, with no provenance, is of little value archaeologically. It has remained with me in the south of England, creating huge interest when shared with my audiences at talks about my years on Lewis. Few people have the opportunity to hold in their hands an object created over 4000 years ago! However, at the time of writing I have arranged for its return to Lewis, for display in the museum at Ravenspoint, about five miles from where it was discovered.

CHAPTER 40

AN AXE FOUND WITH
ITS WOODEN HAFT

One lunch hour in April 1982, in the Biology Staff Room of the Nicolson Institute, I was looking over my lesson notes for the afternoon, when one of my colleagues told me that there was a call for me. It proved to be from the offices of the *Stornoway Gazette*, specifically from Sam Maynard, the paper's award-winning chief photographer.

Sam told me that *'some people out on Point have found another stone axe while peat cutting. It seems that it still has its wooden handle. Is this unusual?'.* Excitedly I replied *'Unusual, it's virtually unheard of'.* I later learnt that the only similar item already exhibited in Edinburgh was a shrivelled remnant of a wooden axe haft, found at Coll in the nineteen-twenties.

Sam was about to visit the family to photograph the find – would I go with him? When I explained the request to my colleagues, they offered to cover my afternoon classes. Sam soon arrived in the little van with the *Gazette* logo and we headed off at alarming speed over the narrow neck of land leading onto the Point peninsula. In Shulishader, we were shown into the immaculately decorated lounge of a modern croft-house. Mrs Macmillan, with no regard for her deep-pile carpet, laid down a muddy-looking plastic bundle.

Opening up the bundle, the axe was revealed – one of my clearest memories of all my archaeological experiences. The axehead, still coated with a thin layer of black peat, appeared to be of high quality. The haft was also blackened, but clearly a skilled piece of woodwork. However, it was in five pieces.

The Macmillans explained that as they had cut the peat, a piece of wood appeared in each section. They thought little of it, as pieces of tree branch near the peat base are not uncommon. However, when they hit stone with the next cut they started to investigate, and realised that they had found a stone axe.

Remembering my previously published comments, they carefully collected the pieces of wood from the cut peats, covered them in damp cloth and wrapped them in polythene. Had they not had the presence of mind to do this, the handle would already have started to deteriorate. I explained that such a find was exceedingly rare and that the wooden handle needed to be taken to a conservation laboratory as soon as possible.

While Sam was taking the photo, I used the Macmillan's phone to call the National Museum. A member of staff in the labs was equally excited - *'If you can get it on the earliest flight from Stornoway to Glasgow we will have a van ready to collect it'*. In fact Calum and Kirsteen's father took it with him on the family's return flight to Glasgow the next morning.

A few days after the find, Trevor Cowie and Niall Sharples visited the Macmillan's peat bank to be shown the exact location from which the axe was extracted. They took samples and surveyed the area. The matter was out of my hands, but having been the go-between at a crucial stage, I maintained a proprietary interest in 'the Shulishader Axe'.

When Sam Maynard and I first saw the axe at Shulishader,
he took this photo with the Macmillan children and their cousins on
a visit from Glasgow. So Kirsteen Macleod (9), Anne Macmillan (3),
Iain Angus Macmillan (6) and Calum Macleod (14) all appeared
on the front page of the Gazette dated April 24th 1982.

I was pleased to see the first photograph of the axe, cleaned and the
peat-preserved wood conserved in the laboratory. The craftsmanship of
the woodworker who had made the handle was obvious (unlike the *Blue
Peter* mock-up!). Both the axehead and wooden haft appeared to have
been in new or nearly-new condition. The axe may have been a prestige,
rather than a practical, object, perhaps for ceremonial use by an important individual. It is more likely to have been a ritual deposit than an
accidental abandonment.

The stone of the axehead was identified as porcellanite from an axe
factory in present-day County Antrim, so provided evidence of trading
from the north of Ireland. The haft was found to be composed of rosa-
ceous wood, from plants such as wild apple or pear, quince or hawthorn.

161

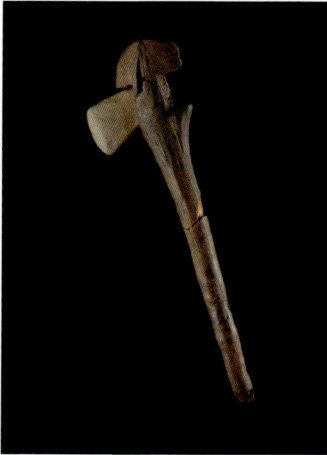

Pollen from this group had been found in local peat samples, so the wood for the haft could have been of island origin, probably hawthorn.

Radiocarbon dating of the wood gave a probable date between 3490 BC and 2910 BC. Only ten other prehistoric axe hafts have been found in Britain; the shrivelled one from Coll, found in the 1920s, has been radiocarbon dated recently, also giving an age of about 5000 years.

The Shulishader Axe became an important exhibit in the National Museum's Early People display. Much later, it appeared briefly in an episode of Alice Roberts's TV series 'Digging for Britain'. But I first saw it again in London in 2022, when it was on loan to the British Museum. In the temporary exhibition 'The World of Stonehenge', displayed in a climate-controlled box, it was the star exhibit among many dozens of stone tools from across Britain.

CHAPTER 41

POLLEN REVEALS A STORY
OF CHANGING VEGETATION

Back in 1976 we amazed our neighbours by going out with a peat iron on a bright frosty morning in November! We were accompanied by John Barber from the Central Excavation Unit. The purpose of our visit was to extract a 'peat column' for laboratory analysis.

The initial observation had been made months earlier by Angus Morrison, our local postman, while cutting his peats. His banks were on a low lying peninsula, jutting southwards from the village of Callanish into Loch Ceann Hulavig. In several banks, he had noticed that, as the peat was cut back each year, more and more stones were revealed, lying in a rough line. It gave the impression of a collapsed wall, perhaps dating from time before peat had started to grow. We were hopeful that these walls might be the field boundaries of Neolithic farms; if so, it would have been the first find relating to the lives of people contemporary with the Callanish Stones.

In another peat bank there was a deposit of branches and twigs at the bottom of the peat. It seemed similar to the well-researched brushwood trackways constructed by ancient man in the peatlands of Somerset. We surveyed the 'stone walls' and the 'trackway' already exposed by peat cuttings. Using aerial photographs of the peninsula, we plotted the positions of the features.

After a chat to members of the Lewis Sub-Aqua Club, several divers searched for further walls under the waters of Loch Ceann Hulavig, but they were frustrated by very murky conditions. The search led to local rumours of an 'underwater village'!

Extracting a Peat Column

The professionals in Edinburgh expressed an interest in the details that we had sent them, initially resulting in the visit of John Barber. By cutting back the peat a little from the existing face, it was possible to draw a measured section through the wall. Careful investigation produced a disappointment – the lowest stones were set *in* the peat, not on the underlying clay. As the Callanish circles were constructed before the peat started to grow, the walls were obviously later than the circles.

However, the extraction of a peat column went ahead. John pushed half-metre long metal boxes, known as Kubiena tins, into the peat face, one above the other. We dug the tins out, with the peat samples intact inside, then wrapped them in polythene to keep them damp during transportation to a laboratory. But this was not the first peat sample taken locally.

Peat Samples from Gisla

At Gisla a similar column of samples had been obtained where peat was three metres deep and undisturbed by cutting. The samples were studied in 1976 at Cambridge University Botany School by H J B Birks, assisted by Barbara Madsen (of Michigan University visiting on a Churchill Scholarship). Slices from the column had been radiocarbon dated at a different laboratory, so that palaeo-botanists Birks and Madsen knew the approximate age of each section as they examined it for pollen.

Although pollen grains are microscopic they are very tough. Like wood, they can be preserved in the peat for thousands of years. Peat cutters finding wood at the bottom of a peat bank often concluded that Lewis was once covered with forest. Pollen tells a different story.

Pollen grains of many plants are carried, often in vast quantities, by the wind. Grains from each species are different from those of any other species. Numerous samples of peat, sliced from the column, were studied at Cambridge. Each slice contained up to 700 pollen grains and every single grain had to be identified. Around fifty different species of plant were recognised.

The most noticeable result was that, throughout thousands of years, trees never formed a large proportion of the vegetation. What tree pollen was found came mostly from birch and hazel.

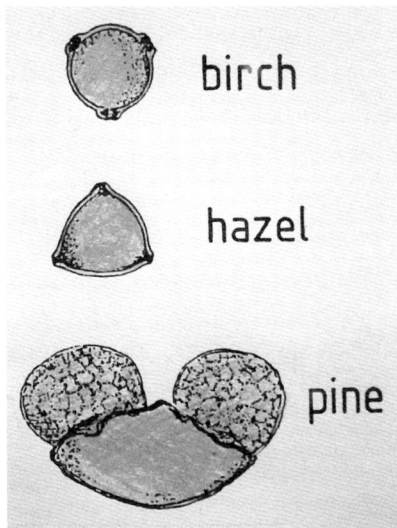

Pollen grains from different plants are identified by their distinctive shapes as seen under a microscope.

Until about 300 BC, the area's landscape was largely grassland and heathland. Small copses of birch and hazel occurred here and there, with clumps of willow. As in Orkney, Shetland and Caithness, the sparseness of tree cover was probably due to frequent westerly gales. With few grazing animals, dense areas of fern, angelica and meadowsweet – such as still occur on islands in lochs – were fairly common. The Gisla samples contained little evidence of human activity. Trees may have been burnt by settlers in about 2000 BC and corn was grown in the area between AD 300 and 800.

Excavation at 'Leobag'

In June 1979, we joined Trevor Cowie's team from the Central Excavation Unit to investigate the possible 'field walls' and 'trackways' in the area that we had previously surveyed. Over three weeks, several trenches were opened, exposing further stretches of wall.

Finding a name for the site proved a problem. Enquiries in the village revealed that there was no generally-accepted local name for the low peninsula. The nearest name on the Ordnance Survey map was that of the adjoining muddy creek — Tob nan Leobag (the bay of the flounders). It was decided to use this, obviously dropping 'Tob' from the name of a land feature. For better or worse, the site became entered into Scotland's archaeological archives as CALLANISH-LEOBAG. A sort of bilingual pun arose as a second justification for the name. *'Leobag — flounder — it's what you do in the damp peat'*.

Trevor Cowie's work confirmed that the stone wails were field boundaries of a late Bronze Age farm, dating from about 1200 BC. The walls extended into an area now covered by the high tides — a clear indication of lower sea levels in those days. The supposed 'trackway' proved to be a natural wood deposit.

Excavation at Leobag exposed the root system and chopped-off trunk of a large tree, probably felled by Late Bronze Age farmers.

However, the most significant results from Leobag were those from pollen analysis, new samples taken in 1979 supplementing those taken by John Barber in 1976. The analysis was carried out by Dr Sjoerd Bohncke, starting work in Scotland while employed by the CEU, but completing it at his lab in Amsterdam. The research produced much interesting information, revealed in Patrick Ashmore's comprehensive report on his excavations at the Callanish Stones.

Leobag in the Mesolithic

In the lowest levels of the Callanish-Leobag peat column, dating from over 8000 years ago, 75% of the pollen preserved was from birch trees. Imagine the area before rising sea levels had flooded Loch Ceann Hulavig. The inlet now bounded by Callanish, Garynahine, Linshader and the Grimersta Estate was then mostly dry land. The pollen results conjure a picture of a fertile valley, thickly clothed with birch trees – more wooded than suggested by the Gisla results. Spores from ferns indicated that many species grew beneath the trees. Yellow cow-wheat flowers and climbing honeysuckle added a colourful touch to the clearings.

A little higher up the column (so of a more recent date), there was a dramatic drop in the amount of birch pollen, down from 75% to 14% over a fairly short period. This could have been a natural occurrence, but fragments of charcoal are found at the same level, strongly suggesting that the woodland was destroyed by fire – perhaps deliberate burning. Charcoal was radiocarbon dated to around 6400 BC, the Mesolithic period, an early date for possible human activity in the Outer Hebrides.

Mesolithic (Middle Stone Age) peoples lived in semi-nomadic groups of hunters and gatherers. They had no knowledge of agriculture and had not invented the stone axe. They may have been burning woodland to open it up in the course of their hunting activities. Mesolithic tools are quite distinctive, typically consisting of tiny flakes of flint or other stone, some flakes being fitted as the tips of arrows used in hunting.. However, sites been long known on Jura and Oronsay, and despite the probable disappearance of coastal settlements with rising sea levels, there is increasing evidence of sites around the western shores of Scotland.

Let us imagine Mesolithic tribes paddling their skin boats into an East Loch Roag which was narrower and shallower than it is today. Perhaps they had 'island-hopped' from Jura over generations of improving climate — making northward migration practical. The birch woodland was an attractive area for settlement. The tribes hunted the wild animals, large and small, for meat and skins. No doubt they also gathered wild fruits and seeds, fungi and shellfish as an essential addition to their diet. Eventually, they set the forest alight, perhaps to drive out a declining game population. With their woodland resource destroyed, they no doubt moved on elsewhere. However, it is important to realise that archaeologists can never accept this as more than a plausible story unless actual Mesolithic tools are found in the area.

First Farmers at Leobag

From about 4000 BC, further marked changes in the vegetation suggest the arrival and expansion of the first farming communities in the area. Pollen levels of birch, willow and rowan declined, suggesting a new phase of tree clearance. At about the same time, cereal pollen appeared, indicating arable cultivation. While small areas of woodland remained, most were cleared by around 1500 BC. After this date, the pollen was dominated by grasses, cereals, weeds of arable cultivation and plants of pastureland such as white clover and tormentil. Deterioration of soil and climate caused the area to be abandoned for a while. When it was settled again, heather-covered moorland dominated the vegetation.

Field Walls Near the Stones

In 1999 and 2000, the Calanais Fields Project was directed by Catherine Flitcroft and Melanie Johnson of the University of Edinburgh. They excavated on land immediately to the south-west of the Callanish Stones, land that slopes downwards towards Loch Roag. Clear evidence was found for agricultural activity in the Late Bronze Age / Early Iron Age, including field walls, clearance cairns and other structures. The inlet of the loch separating this area from Leobag may have been dry land at the time, and perhaps divided into fields. This idea was supported by finds of eroding walls at high tide level by the SCAPE community archaeology project (chapter 26).

CHAPTER 42

A NEVER COMPLETED NOVEL

In the 1980s, I wrote the first seven chapters of a novel, *'Awake the Stones'*. It was planned as a fictionalised version of the major excavations at Callanish in 1980 and 1981, when a group of artists camped nearby, seeing themselves as 'monitors' of the archaeologists (chapter 18).

In two early chapters, Marcie Compton, the director of the dig, was arguing at sunset among the Stones with Mick Stevenson, the most outspoken of the artists; while Barbara Macey, one of the dig volunteers, was chatting to Calum Maciver, a shy young Lewisman, on the ferry from Ullapool. I wrote of my fictional characters that *they had little idea of the depth of the relationship which would be forced on their disparate teams by events which had occurred in the depths of prehistory'*.

Influenced by recent finds of stone axeheads and by the results of pollen analysis, I planned to tell the story of a trader in axeheads visiting Neolithic Lewis for the first time, interspersing this with the twentieth-century chapters. However, I had no confidence that I could sustain the plot and the characters for a full-length novel — or to write believably of Neolithic ceremonies. I've since always considered myself a writer of non-fiction.

A Few Excerpts From Chapter 4 — *Hort The Trader*

A flimsy-looking, but carefully constructed, boat of skin and wooden laths sailed up to the head of a long sea-loch. There were four men on board, using paddles and a simple form of sail to propel the little vessel. ... ...

Hort looked around at the bleak and rocky landscape. ... ... He realised that he was now on the last stage of his epic journey, an expedition which would be beyond the imaginations of most of his contemporaries. He was a trader in stone axeheads – a sort of 'commercial traveller' of his day. Such men were inveterate journeyers in an age when few men knew more than the immediate territories of their own tribes. ... ...

He knew many temples in the land, knew of the efforts made for generations to complete the hallowed circles, understood the divine need for the work – but the whole idea of 'Hanging Stones' [Stonehenge] had to be the work only of fertile imaginations, or so he believed.

Almost equal in its reputation, and equally remote from the areas Hort generally visited, was the Great Winged Temple*, across the sea far to the north and west. He had talked, long ago, with another trader who had visited it himself. Hort well remembered his enthusiastic descriptions of the Temple and the welcome he had received from the tribes there. Hort had decided to make the Winged Temple the final objective of his current journey. ... ...

They climbed from the shore to the rolling uplands, a grassy countryside with dense patches of fern. Copses of rowan, birch and hazel broke up the landscape and no doubt provided shelter for plenty of game. ... ...

After a trek of several hours, they topped a rise and stood overlooking a broad valley. Hort was speechless, overcome by the splendour of the view.

As the group of travellers moved lower, a rocky ridge within the valley seemed to rise up to form a new horizon. Hort gasped with astonishment. All along the ridge stood the huge stones which made up the famed Temple.

---

* In ancient Greece, Eratosthenes may have been referring to Callanish with its east and west rows when writing of a 'winged' temple in the far north.

The stones stood out from the sunset in the western sky. It was a moment he would never forget and one which he would retell, lovingly and frequently, around many firesides when he returned to southern lands.

CHAPTER 43

WESTERN ISLES CONFERENCE IN EDINBURGH

On October 29th 1983, I joined around one hundred other Scottish archaeologists in a lecture theatre at Edinburgh University. The title of the one-day conference, organised jointly by the University and the Society of Antiquaries of Scotland, was *Neolithic and Bronze Age Settlement in the Western Isles*.

Most of the speakers were experts whom we had met on the Isle of Lewis in previous years, and many of their talks included thanks for our

171

efforts. It occurred to me that the conference could not have happened in the same form but for our initial work on Callanish, Leobag, Dalmore and other sites, all of which had been followed up by the professionals.

'Archaeology on the Isle of Lewis'

The latest issue of the *Scottish Archaeological Gazette* was available at the conference. It contained our five-page article with the above title, summarising many of our activities over the previous eight years. The following paragraphs are verbatim from this 1983 article –

> *'We think we can claim to have increased archaeological awareness on an island where many people were almost ashamed of their past.*
>
> *Why dwell, they felt, on the Clearances and the tacksmen, the official suppression of Gaelic and the squalor of primitive housing, now that crofters have smart modern homes with colour TV and two freezers inside and a gleaming Datsun parked outside.*
>
> *The thought of a prehistoric heritage, reaching back thousands of years to a time when Callanish was a great communal centre and at least the equal of anything to be found elsewhere in Britain, was a new idea to many people.'*

Machair v. Black Lands

A theme of the conference was the relationship between the habitation sites of early peoples and the known or supposed environment at the time. In particular, a major question for the speakers was the relative importance of the machair and of the 'black lands' – the moorland of pre-peat days.

Iain Crawford, director of many seasons of digs on North Uist, said that it was artificial to consider the land types separately, as they tended to be complementary resources. In Neolithic and Bronze Age times, the machair was a 'resource to be used up to the hilt', with the small strips having an importance out of all proportion to their size. The black soils were a dependence of the machair, and could not have supported separate settlements on any substantial scale. However, 'ceremonial' sites, like the Callanish circles, were generally situated on the black lands.

Eilean an Tighe

Ian Crawford also suggested that a re-appraisal might be needed for the Eilean an Tighe site on North Uist. Excavated in 1937 by Sir Lindsay Scott, the report was eventually published in 1953 by his son, Neil Scott, after Sir Lindsay's death.

Eilean an Tighe (island of the house) is within a freshwater loch, Loch nan Geireann. The ruinous 'house' had been examined, decades earlier, by Erskine Beveridge who had found prehistoric tools and pottery.

Scott's 1953 report in *PSAS* was entitled *'Eilean an Tighe — a Pottery Workshop of the Second Millenium BC'*. The bulk of the finds in the dig were potsherds, representing perhaps as many as 365 pots. Charcoal and flint flakes had been found, as well as polished stone tools, interpreted as implements for decorating and burnishing pots. Piles of clay were considered to be unused raw material for more pots. 'Hearths', 'flues' and 'ovens' were clearly marked on plans in the report – interpretation rather than objective recording.

Crawford found Scott's 'pottery workshop' interpretation, plausible in 1953, difficult to accept in 1983, partly as such sites were so rarely found. No other pottery sites were known for that period from anywhere in Europe, and none from the Western Isles for any date.

He pointed out that the Neolithic settlement had developed on what was probably a peninsula rather than an island at that time. Its situation in Loch nan Geireann gave it access to one of the best salmon runs in North Uist and this could have been a major reason for the choice of site.

Callanish Connections

Patrick Ashmore's talk on the Callanish Stones dealt mostly with their wider links across Scotland. Of the pottery fragments found, about three-quarters were of a style found widely, rather than of a distinctive Hebridean style.

Some stone tools were made from a type of rock found on Skye. The shape of the Callanish circle (Professor Thom's 'type A flattened circle') is the same as that of Temple Wood in Argyll. There are megaliths at Callanish, at Brodgar and Stenness on Orkney, and at Machrie Moor on Arran that are of similar shape though of very different geological origins.

Patrick envisaged connections between communities on different islands, maintained by vessels coasting between Orkney and the Argyll islands, as well as criss-crossing The Minch.

Other Speakers

Unfortunately, it seems that the lectures given at this conference were never published in book form. However, several chapters in this book are at least partly based on notes or recordings that I took at the time.

- Niall Sharples gave a report of his recently completed work at Dalmore (chapter 44).
- Trevor Cowie spoke on erosion and the Barvas machair (chapter 48) and also on Leobag (chapter 41).
- Derek Simpson described his excavations at Northton (chapter 33).

CHAPTER 44

DALMORE – A 'REDEPOSITED' SITE?

While living at Callanish, our nearest beach was Dalmore, a great place for a family visit, even if the sun was not shining and it was too cool for a paddle. Walking on the sands on the day after a storm, the breaking waves were always spectacular. Our children enjoyed clambering over the rocks at either end of the beach. After a while, we realised that there was an area of shingle at the top of the shore where potsherds, discarded shells, pieces of bone or other ancient artefacts might be found. Casually, in the course of family visits, we started a small collection.

We learnt that there was earlier evidence of prehistoric occupation. In 1905, a bone borer, perhaps used in the preparation of skins, was found and a record of it was sent to Edinburgh, its present whereabouts unknown. Fifty years later, a schoolboy, James Macarthur, found a 'highly polished bone awl', which was purchased by the National Museum. Also in the 1950s, a surface collection of finds was made by Robert Macleod. A stone axehead was presented to Shawbost Museum, other material went to a mainland museum, while a third bone borer was retained in private hands.

In 1978, the archaeologists of the Coastal Erosion Survey visited Dalmore. Trevor Cowie and his colleagues decided that, although the site was the remains of a prehistoric midden, it was of little archaeological interest. The artefacts had been redeposited by wind, waves or a stream, not lying where its users had left them, thousands of years ago.

In February 1979, two Council workmen called at our house to show us a 'stone tractor seat', actually a prehistoric saddle quern. They had found it while working on the construction of a new section of sea wall, intended to protect the extension to the cemetery, the smaller CEMY shown on the plan overleaf. (Island cemeteries are situated on sandy machair in preference to damp peaty soils.)

For the rest of that month, Margaret kept a watching brief. Her only finds were groups of animal bones. The seawall, once completed, altered the pattern of sand movement on the beach. This resulted in the exposure of further prehistoric material at high tide level. In June 1979, I found the first piece of patterned pottery among midden material on the beach.

We contacted the archaeologists who happened to be working elsewhere on Lewis. They examined the Dalmore midden, concurring with the previous opinion that the material was re-deposited. Perhaps the nearby stream, the Allt Garbh, had washed the midden to its present position. Therefore, careful recording of the position of each find was not necessary. We were encouraged to follow the midden layer on the beach and recover any artefacts present.

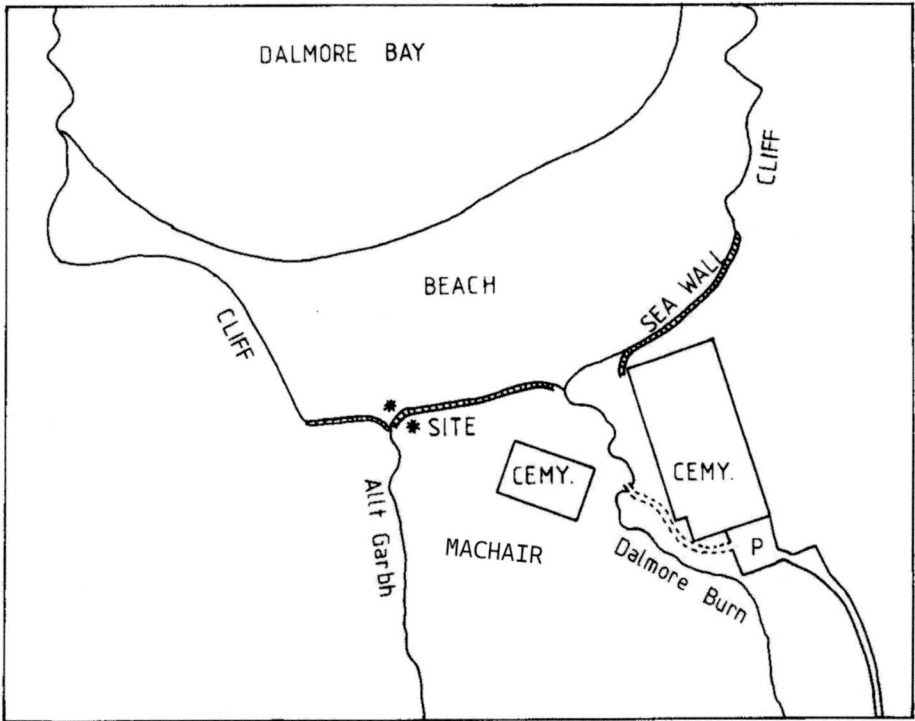

Plan of Dalmore beach area. The upper asterisk marks the area on the beach examined before the seawall collapsed – stages 1 and 2. The lower asterisk shows the position of the deep excavation in the machair, following that collapse – stage 3 onwards.

Stage One

Thus began the first phase of Margaret's work on site. From 1979 onwards, family visits to the beach were accompanied by small-scale excavation. The first bone awl caused us a great deal of excitement and the first stone arrowhead was an even greater thrill. By January 1981, the collection was already extensive enough to justify professional examination. Trevor Cowie from the National Museum spent a week at our home classifying the finds.

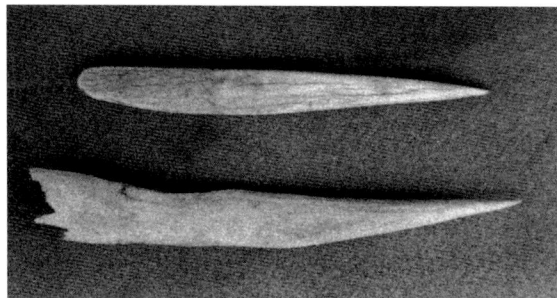

A few finds from the midden excavated at Dalmore. Sharpened bone tools may have been used to pierce holes in leather, or perhaps to inscribe decorative patterns on clay pots before firing. The finely-shaped quartz arrowhead was just one item in the large lithics collection, while the potsherd was among the, also very numerous, collection of Beaker Period pottery (scale in cm).

They included numerous decorated fragments of pottery, barbed-and-tanged arrowheads of both quartz and flint, bone pins, quern stones, quantities of shell, animal bones, etc. Most remarkably, one small piece of bone was both shaped and painted, a unique find (more details in chapter 46).

Stage Two

In 1982, Margaret began much more extensive removal of blown sand from above the prehistoric layer. She suspected that the site might not be entirely re-deposited, but that remnants of walls were present. This led to the calling in of various expert second opinions. The answer was always the same – there is no cash available for a professional team to take over, so try to gather all the finds you can, before a storm destroys the whole deposit.

From August to October, Margaret toiled on the beach, sometimes with helpers, more often accompanied only by gulls, sheep, rabbits, circling eagles and the occasional curious seal! Shovel away the white blown sand, trowel out the layer just above the chocolate-brown prehistoric soil, sieve it for finds. Spend each evening sorting and classifying. At each stage, a photographic record of the site was kept, and plans of any possible structures drawn up.

By early October, the task was complete. It seemed very likely that much more of the site lay buried behind the seawall and there it would remain undisturbed. The storms could do their worst without damaging any prehistoric remains ... or so we thought.

Storm, Autumn 1982

We had reckoned without a violent storm changing the course of the Dalmore Burn. Now running eastwards across the top of the beach, it scoured sand away from the new seawall. The wall bulged here, split there, then collapsed along much of its length. The machair and even the cemetery extension were under possible threat of further erosion.

In mid-November, contractors for Comhairle nan Eilean started work with a large mechanical excavator. The repair involved digging huge holes in the machair behind the collapsed wall. The intention was to anchor the wall, using horizontal straining wires to connect it to large cast-iron anchor plates buried further back in the machair.

Stage Three

In the hole nearest to our former beach excavations, the contractors revealed large areas of tumbled stones. Following a visit to the site by the Chairman and Convenor of the Comhairle, Margaret was permitted to continue excavating in this most interesting area, while the reconstruction of the wall continued along the rest of its length.

Nevertheless, there always seemed to be a deadline, after which the excavation area would need to be re-filled with sand. In the site notebook, time and again the note appears 'two more days only'. But it's an ill wind that blows no good, and materials ordered by the contractors failed to arrive, delaying their work, but extending the time available for excavation.

Despite awful weather conditions, the work continued throughout the darkest days of winter with frequent gale-force winds. Niall Sharples, who later took over the excavation, made these apt comments on Margaret's work – *'some considerable expenditure of effort in circumstances which could at best be described as appalling … very real dangers involved in working in deep trenches in unstable sand'*. She had become quite obsessive about the project.

However, the results were remarkable, with finds more prolific than ever. Each evening, these needed partial sorting and the day's records had to be written up. Our sun-lounge gradually filled with stacks of wooden tomato boxes (174 of them!) that I had sourced from Stornoway's small supermarkets. Teaching full-time, and abiding by local attitudes to the Sabbath in the dark days of winter, I was able to visit Dalmore only on Saturdays. Weekends also gave me the opportunity to photograph the more interesting finds.

Structures Need to Be Excavated

In mid-December, Patrick Ashmore flew to Lewis to examine the Dalmore site. But it was late January before we finally persuaded the Ancient Monuments department that the site needed to be included in their budget. Our plans and photographs at last provided convincing evidence that the site was not just 'redeposited' but included structures.

The remains of a wall – which at last convinced the professionals
that our excavation contained Bronze Age structures
and was not just a redeposited site.

If these proved to be the walls of a Beaker period house, Dalmore would prove to be of national, rather than local, significance. Only about a dozen sites in the British Isles had revealed Beaker period houses. In mid-February, we closed the site for six weeks, pending the arrival of the professional team. They intended to *gauge the extent and significance of the preserved deposits and to try and obtain a context for the by now large collections obtained from the site*.

The Professionals Take Over

Of the reports presented at the Edinburgh conference, the most topical was on Dalmore. Only six months after the completion of his four-week excavation there, Niall Sharples of the National Museum was able to give a reasonably detailed story of a prehistoric house. He distinguished five distinct phases of activity during occupation over several centuries.

Dalmore, Phase One

Little is known about the earliest structure, which seems to have been an oval stone wall, enclosing a large area, with no reason to suppose that it was a roofed house.

Dalmore, Phase Two

Next, a wall was built across the oval, creating a smaller, roughly circular house, presumably with a roof. Pottery sherds, bones and tools recovered from the floor provided clues to the lives of the inhabitants (see next chapter). Charcoal fragments embedded in the floor no doubt came from a fire. There were at least sixteen storage pits dug into the floor, a known feature of some prehistoric houses. One pit proved to have a paved bottom and partly stone-lined sides.

The rest of the earlier oval continued in use as *an external activity area* … a yard. A six-foot long stone-walled passage connected the house and the yard.

Dalmore, Phase Three

After a major rebuilding, the interior of the house was made even smaller and roughly rectangular in shape. In one wall, three courses of stone were still intact. It seems possible that this structure was not in continuous use, but occupied intermittently, perhaps seasonally.

An Observation

I'd like to record a personal observation about the Dalmore site, which may relate to its possibly seasonal use. Niall had never visited the site in winter, so this might not have been obvious to him.

There are cliffs and hills to the east and south of the site; the sun never rises above them in the depths of winter. The sun may be shining brightly further along the beach, while the site remains in deep shade. Given a more extensive machair area at Dalmore when the sea level was lower, and even accepting that the climate was better then, why should prehistoric man have chosen to live in a sun-less spot throughout the winter?

Dalmore, Phase Four

When the rectangular house fell out of use, it silted up with sand. Even in this sand, some occupation debris was found. Perhaps people were occasionally 'camping out' in the ruins.

Dalmore, Phase Five

Above this layer was another of water-rounded boulders, suggesting that the Allt Garbh became diverted across the site. This could explain the initial finds of tools and pottery on the beach, washed down by the stream. There was some confusing evidence of human constructional activity.

Finds and Conclusions

There were numerous finds from each phase, with location and stratification carefully recorded. Most of the earlier finds had not had their positions strictly recorded, as we had frequently been assured that the material was 'redeposited'. In 2025, a full report on the finds is still 'forthcoming'.

In his Interim Report, Niall Sharples called Dalmore a *settlement of*

considerable importance to our understanding of the prehistory of Lewis ...
Previous sites of the Beaker period had been known and excavated in the
Western Isles, the most well known being Rosinish and Northton, but few
sites with continuity into the later Early Bronze Age are known. The only
possible example is the nearby ritual complex at Callanish'.

CHAPTER 45

LIFE IN BRONZE AGE DALMORE

A few months before Niall Sharples started work at Dalmore, I had
boldly headlined one of my Gazette articles 'DALMORE - A NEW
CHAPTER IN BRITISH PREHISTORY'. I had felt able to give
a popular account of what life was like for the inhabitants of Dalmore,
based on the evidence of artefacts already found ... but with no know-
ledge of Niall's five phases. The following has been slightly adapted from
that article.

Around 4,000 years ago, a group of people, perhaps a few families, lived
at Dalmore. The sea level was lower then, with machair extending below
the present lowest tide-line, so their homes were not as close to the
beach as the site appears today.

From the bone fragments in their middens, we know that they kept
sheep and cattle and used them as a source of food. They hunted deer
and ate venison; dogs may have been used in the hunt. A fifth species
whose bones are found is the pig, but there is no way of telling whether
their pork came from wild or domesticated pigs. Meat was probably
cooked on spits over an open fire, but also by the use of 'pot-boilers' (as
at Eoropie, chapter 37).

Although the little community lived close to the sea, they do not seem to have been fishermen — fish bones are rare in the midden. But shell-fish were eaten. Vast numbers of limpet shells suggest that these rather tough creatures were a major part of the diet. Oysters, mussels and winkles were also eaten.

In addition to animal husbandry, hunting and the gathering of shell-fish, crops were grown. We know that they cultivated cereals from the finds of three saddle querns, used to grind grain. (This was later confirmed by Niall's find of a few dozen carbonised cereal grains.) No doubt the flour produced in this way was baked into some form of bread, but this must remain guesswork.

Tools for many purposes were made from stone and bone. Ovoid pebbles of a size convenient to hold in the hand were used as hammer-stones and are recognisable by their battered ends. Their exact use is uncertain.

Polished stone axeheads were precious tools and are thus not often found in middens. The Dalmore collection includes the blade end of a broken axehead, which we found about a week after the find of the Shulishader axe.

The flaking of stone to make tools is a well-known prehistoric tech-nology. In most parts of Britain, flint was the favoured stone, but it is uncommon in north-west Scotland. Nevertheless, well over one hundred pieces of flaked flint were found at Dalmore, including eighteen scrapers. More commonly, quartz tools were used. This white stone is abundant locally, but it is more difficult than flint to shape into tools. It seems clear that the Dalmore community made their own quartz tools, as finds include the cores from which flakes were struck, also several thousand quartz flakes discarded as waste.

A third type of flaked stone was used at Dalmore, provisionally iden-tified as mylonite – of which more in chapter 47.

Thirty scrapers, in all three types of stone, were found. They may have served a variety of purposes, but it is easy to imagine a scraper, held between finger and thumb, being used to remove pieces of fat from a sheep or cattle skin, preparing it for use in making garments.

Four quartz arrowheads may be considered unfinished or sub-standard. However, the six finished arrowheads reveal the great deal of skill required for their manufacture. The best one is perfectly symmetrical, a functional object, but also the most obviously attractive find to a non-archaeologist. Presumably arrowheads were made in some quantity and bound to wooden shafts for use in hunting deer.

I have already mentioned that three bone awls or borers were found at Dalmore many years ago. We found no less than thirty-four further bone tools. Most are sharply pointed and were probably used for making holes in skins before they were stitched together for clothing. Several are highly polished from regular use. Other bone tools may have been used for decorating clay pots before firing.

The early inhabitants of Dalmore probably made and used functional and artistic wooden and leather objects – but wood and leather decay, so unsurprisingly no trace was found. Bronze also corrodes, so the find of a single tiny fragment is the only indication that this was a metal-using community.

Pottery, however, remains well-preserved. About 1500 pieces of decorated pottery were recovered at Dalmore, and many are richly patterned. (The later dig by Niall Sharples revealed a change in ceramic styles through the changes in the building.) Our pottery collection from Dalmore was described as '*a large and important assemblage of great significance*', not just locally but nationwide.

Our interest in a possible habitation site at Dalmore arose from a wish to know where and how people lived at the time that the Callanish Stones were a living monument. While detailed study of the Dalmore pottery is still pending, and pottery found at Callanish was mostly fragmentary, the same styles were found at both sites. What is more, an enclosure excavated next to the circle at Callanish (a feature not obvious to the casual visitor) has definite similarities in structure to the Bronze Age house at Dalmore.

To the way of life described, we can speculatively add … walking nine miles to attend ceremonies at the great Temple.

CHAPTER 46

THE UNIQUE DALMORE BONE 'RULER'

I was sorting through the pieces of bone in Margaret's most recent collection of finds at Dalmore, removing loose sand with a paint brush. Most pieces were random scraps, probably food waste, but now and again I put one aside for further examination and photography, mostly pieces sharpened into points for use as tools.

Then I found something really remarkable. A little over an inch long, the piece of bone had been shaped, giving it a roughly square cross-section and a squared-off end. Much more unusual – and even then I thought, *is this unique?* – a distinctive pattern was 'painted' on two of the sides.

Some years later Margaret gave a detailed account of the 'Dalmore bone'. It is formed from a lower leg bone - metacarpal or metatarsal - from sheep or goat, possibly deer. The surviving piece is 34 mm long, but it is thought likely to have been around 100 mm long before breakage. The outer surface had been shaped as already described, while it retained its natural hollow.

Similar pieces of shaped bone have been recorded from Balbirnie, Dalgety Bay and Patrickholm, but none of these shared the Dalmore bone's unique feature – colouration. Triangles were marked on two adjacent faces and coloured with a red dye or paint. Our initial impression had been that it might have been some kind of ruler.

Two ancient wooden rods from Denmark are thought to have been intended for use as rulers. Notches on a hazel rod from a Bronze Age site in East Jutland divide it into fifths – 1/5, 1/5, 2/5, 1/5. An oak rod from the Iron Age site of Borre Fen has cuts on one edge dividing it into eight equal sections.

Professor Thom believed that stone circles were set out using a unit

The unique 'bone ruler' from Dalmore. The
triangular markings on two adjacent edges were
distinctly coloured a dusty red when found.
Unfortunately the colour faded when exposed
to air and light and no colour photographs
taken before that seem to have survived. (In
fact, I mostly photographed finds in black-and-
white as publications then rarely used colour.)

that he called the Megalithic Yard, equal to 2.72 feet or 0.83 metres. He
also suggested that the makers of cupmarks used a Megalithic Inch (MI),
one-fortieth of a MY. The subdivisions on both of the Danish rods have
lengths which can be considered as 8 MI.

The markings on the Dalmore bone were measured photogrammetri-
cally by Dr P J Scott. Four triangles, taken together, measure just over
20 mm, which is close to Thom's supposed Megalithic Inch. Possible
uses suggested for the 'ruler' include the design of cup-marks on stone;
or drawing the geometrical design of stone circles in small scale on a
leather 'drawing board'.

Whether or not the Dalmore bone was designed for use as a ruler, as
a shaped bone, decorated with a coloured pattern, it remains a unique
artefact, discovered in our investigations of a 'redeposited midden'.

Festschrift for Professor Thom

Margaret's account of our unique find appeared in *'Records in Stone'*
(1988), a collection of essays in honour of Thom's lifetime of research,
edited by Clive Ruggles. Her essay also transcribed a personal letter that
we had received from the Prof some years earlier. In it he described, in
more detail than published elsewhere, how he had first visited Callanish

on a yachting trip in 1933, and how his observation of the accurate orientation of the south row had inspired him to begin his long-term project of surveying stone circles.

CHAPTER 47

THE MYLONITE MYSTERY

Sometimes, an archaeological problem can be as fascinating as a detective story. And sometimes, a possible solution is provided by an expert from outside the field of archaeology.

As already explained, the excavation at Dalmore uncovered vast quantities of Bronze Age material. Among the bones and shells from the midden there were many flakes of stone. Most numerous were quartz flakes, well over 2,000 of them, the rejects from tool manufacture, carried out by the deliberate flaking of lumps of raw quartz. A few flakes had been chosen as suitable for re-touching. Careful, skilled chipping at the edges of a flake produced a sharp tool - a scraper for cleaning the skins of cattle, sheep or deer; or an arrowhead for hunting. Such tools were found among the rejected flakes.

Quartz was by no means the preferred material for stone tools in prehistoric Britain. In the chalk districts of England, the mining of flint and the preparation of effective flint knives, axes, arrowheads and spear-points was well advanced. Vatersay is one of the very few sources of flint in the west of Scotland. The small flint tools and flakes found at Dalmore, over a hundred of them, were probably sourced from flint pebbles found on the shore.

The 'mylonite mystery' began in 1980 with the find at Dalmore of a finely-shaped arrowhead, which was clearly neither flint nor quartz. My diary entry described it as a *'lovely little pink and green arrowhead'*. The colours were especially noticeable when wet.

A second mysterious find from Dalmore – an arrowhead, its tip broken, of a striped stone provisionally known as mylonite. The object remains in the large lithics collection awaiting study. Scale in cm.

Gradually, as work at Dalmore continued, a collection of scrapers and other tools of this mystery rock was found. The first clue to the nature of the stone came from reading a report on the Northton excavations. I found a mention of 'mylonite scrapers'. Consulting a popular guide to British geology, more colourful than technical, I found an illustration of 'banded mylonite' that appeared to be a good match for the mystery rock. I also found 1930s references to mylonite tools found at Kneep and at nearby Berie in A D Lacaille's excavations.

Derek Simpson, director of the Northton dig in the 1960s, paid a return visit to the island in 1981. He showed Margaret the natural outcrops of mylonite on the beach near the Northton site, thought to be the source of the tools found there. A search then began for other exposures of mylonite rock, but none were found near Dalmore. The most obvious outcrop is the tower of rock on the west side of the main road, just north of Balallan.

Volunteers at the Callanish dig in 1981 were alerted to the possibility of finding mylonite specimens, and around 30 tools of the same substance were recorded in the eventual report.

Thus, at Northton and at Dalmore, at Callanish and at Kneep, prehistoric man used an unusual fine-grained rock for making tools. The making of mylonite tools appears to have been a Hebridean industry, developed in the absence of good supplies of flint. But what is the true nature of the stone? And where was it quarried?

Following the finds at Callanish, the archaeology authorities in Edinburgh handed the mystery over to the geologists. Geoff Collins of the Institute of Geological Sciences undertook the investigation, and his results were first announced at the conference on Western Isles archaeology in October 1983.

A tool from Callanish and a tool from Dalmore had been studied, microscopic examination suggesting that neither were composed of mylonite, but of baked shale. (I should perhaps make it clear that the term 'baked' refers to a natural process in the Earth, back in the dim distances of geological time - not to any technique practised on the stone by prehistoric Man.)

The next question was, where is baked shale found? The first, categorical, statement that could be made was - nowhere on the Long Island. Among the places marked 'Baked Shale' on the geological map were Duntulm and the Bay of Staffin in north Skye. Geoff Collins and a colleague visited the outcrops of baked shale in Skye and took samples back to Edinburgh for analysis.

The tools from Dalmore and Callanish were compared with the rock samples from Duntulm and Staffin. The amounts of 24 different trace elements were checked. All four samples matched, Collins concluding that the tools were made from baked shale from Skye. Rejected flakes had been found at Dalmore, suggesting that tools were made there from rock imported from Skye.

Professor Simpson, wanting clarity on 'mylonite' tools from Northton, agreed at the 1983 conference to provide a sample to the geologists for analysis. A 1986 report claimed that the Northton 'mylonite' was actually banded mudstone, though this has since been disputed.

In 2021 it was stated that minerals including mylonite and banded mudstone (presumably also baked shale) are *poorly understood materials*.

It was suggested that the name *mylonite* should continue in use as a catch-all term for a group of similar rocks. Geological studies are continuing into mylonite and similar rocks.

CHAPTER 48

COASTAL EROSION AND THE BARVAS MACHAIR

In many places around the Western Isles, there is clear evidence that the present sea level is higher than in past centuries. For example, once-cultivated lazy beds are found on the shore, partially submerged by the high spring tides.

The position of the shoreline has been very variable over the millennia. During an Ice Age, much of the water normally in the oceans was 'locked up' in the form of ice, resulting a world sea level much lower than today's. Britain formed a continuous land mass with Europe, while Islay and Jura were part of a land-bridge from Argyll to Ireland. The Western Isles really did form a single 'Long Island' including the present day Monach and Flannan Isles … but conditions were totally arctic!

When the climate became more temperate and the ice

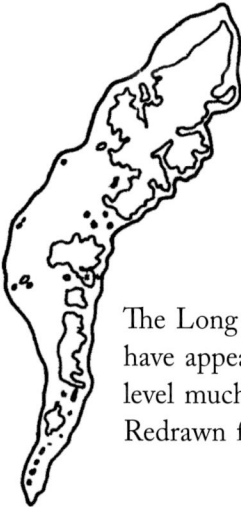

The Long Island as it would have appeared with the sea level much lower than today's. Redrawn from Murray, 1973.

melted — and hunting tribes from Europe followed the retreating ice northwards — vast quantities of water returned to the oceans. At the same time, as the weight of ice was removed, the land slowly rose, but not enough to counteract the rising sea level. The net effect locally was to flood low-lying valleys, producing the indented coastline of the Western Isles – and to submerge sites of early human habitation.

An early Bronze Age cemetery at Rubha an Udail, which Iain Crawford studied in North Uist, is now less than three feet above the level of High Spring Tides. In a lower layer, the rare remains of a Neolithic house are at present-day sea level. It is generally believed that people would not have wanted to live too close to the highest tides; and evidence suggests that the highest tides, even as 'recently' as the Bronze Age, may have been eighteen feet below the present level.

Coastal Erosion

Sea levels continue to rise today, partly as a result of man-made global warming. Erosion of coastal sites is bound to continue — especially as stormy conditions are so common.

There are perhaps three options for an eroding site of archaeological interest. One is to abandon it to the sea in the long term. A second, especially if this would also benefit a local community, is to protect it, expensively, with a sea wall. A less costly answer is a rescue excavation, retrieving finds and information, but not preserving structures, before the site is completely eroded.

In the summer of 1978, archaeologists from the Central Excavation Unit spent several weeks making a Coastal Erosion Survey to assist with such decisions. They walked extensive stretches of the coastline of the Western Isles, examining known sites and recording some previously unknown ones.

At the Edinburgh conference on Western Isles Archaeology in 1983, Trevor Cowie, one of the CEU surveyors, introduced his talk by projecting a slide of the West Side of Lewis taken from space. The Barvas machair showed up clearly as a small patch, lighter in colour than the surrounding moors.

Three Sites at Barvas

The large area of blown sand at Barvas has long been subject to erosion due to a number of very different factors — the action of wind, the burrowing of rabbits, over-grazing by domestic stock, sand extraction and various recreational activities. The surveyors identified several eroding archaeological sites at Barvas. Three were selected as worthy of further study.

The normal pattern of settlement is for successive ages to use the same site, literally building on the ruins of the earlier culture. Archaeologists dig downwards to reach earlier periods, as shown clearly at the Udal in North Uist. So it is a remarkable feature of the 1978/79 studies at Barvas that three *separate* sites seemed to have been occupied in Bronze Age, Iron Age and Norse times.

Iron Age Finds, 1978

The water level in Loch Mor Barvas was exceptionally low in 1978. Stone structures on the northern shore, normally underwater, were temporarily exposed. Undertaking a rescue excavation, we found paved areas within the remains of boulder-built walls. Two hearths, measuring around a metre each way, were each defined by slabs set on edge. We recovered ten hammer-stones and considerable quantities of pottery, as well as worked stone and bone. The area was re-submerged within weeks, and not accessible to examine again till the water level was low in 1984.

On the nearby Atlantic shoreline, wave action had exposed midden material that also contained bones and potsherds. The pottery suggested that there had been Iron Age settlement in the area and, much later in time, medieval occupation.

Norse Site, 1979

In June 1979, Trevor Cowie and his team excavated the other two sites. Not far from the cemetery at the north end of Barvas machair, surface potsherds had been recognised as Norse (Viking) in origin. Excavating through a thick midden deposit, the remains of two stone structures were found.

Each bucket of sand was 'wet-sieved', tipped into a fine-mesh sieve and washed through with a hosepipe or buckets of water. Tools and bone fragments were recovered, but also even tiny objects such as grains of wheat. The many finds made it clear that the Norse inhabitants used a wide variety of resources from sea, shoreline, machair and moors.

Bronze Age Site, 1979

Trevor's team also worked on another area, thought to be a habitation site from the Late Bronze Age. The knoll was excavated, despite its badly eroded state, as such sites are rare in the islands. Fragments of pot were scattered around, along with hammer-stones and scraps of bone. Stones in a rough line suggested remnants of a wall.

The last remnants of a possible house-floor were found, about five metres by four metres. Shells, pottery shards, pieces of antler and bones lay on paved slabs and trampled sand and peat ash.

On several occasions, the archaeologists thought they had found post-holes — traces left by wooden poles that once held up a roof. Closer examination of these features, however, usually revealed that they were caused by rabbits burrowing through the site in modern times!

Life in the Late Bronze Age

Pottery from the eroded Barvas hillock is similar to that from sites on mainland Scotland, sites that match the date of the Adabrock Hoard and of the swords from Dell. These magnificent pieces of metalwork (see chapter 1) tell us very little about how the people lived in the Late Bronze Age. However, the Barvas finds can partly fill that gap.

Mammal bones found were almost all from cattle and sheep, with a few from pigs; all parts of the animals seem to have been eaten. A few fragments of deer bones suggest hunting, but antlers found at the site, no doubt collected for use as tools, were ones that had been naturally cast by the deer.

It appeared that marine resources were being used. A bone from a large whale probably came from an animal cast up on the shore. As is so often the case on island middens, limpets appear to have been the preferred shellfish — a rather tough meal, or collected only as fishing bait?

While fish bones were uncommon on the site as a whole, 775 fragments from one small area of midden were studied at Southampton University. (Modern archaeologists must know where to call upon experts in all sorts of fields!) Many pieces were too small to be recognised, but of those positively identified, 3% were saithe, 26% were ling and 71% were cod. Some of the bones appeared to have come from large fish. While it is possible that, before the sea's resources were heavily fished, larger specimens came nearer the shore, this suggests that Bronze Age peoples ventured several miles out to sea, using hook and line from an open boat.

Apart from the 'beach pebble hammers', the only tools found were sharpened pieces of bone, perhaps used to pierce leather, and a few quartz scrapers. In contrast to the vast amount of material found by wet-sieving at the nearby Norse site, here this method retrieved very few plant remains. Barley grains were identified, however, suggesting that the people may have grown some crops.

To sum up, we now know much more about the early Lewismen who built stone walls around their fields — and who lived at a time when bronze bowls and swords were in use, probably imported from the continent. We know that they kept cows and sheep and a few pigs; they hunted deer and collected antlers; they gathered food from the shore and fished, maybe quite far out to sea. Not a bad collection of information for three weeks' work on a small sand-hill, riddled with rabbit holes!

Later Studies

The Barvas Machair continued to be of interest to archaeologists in more recent decades. Field walls have been found; there was a more detailed erosion survey in 1996; there were further excavations, including recovery of human remains from Bronze Age and Iron Age burials.

Between 2003 and 2013, Mark Elliott, conservator at Museum nan Eilean, assisted by family and friends, field-walked eroding areas on the machair – finding mostly stone artefacts, nearly 7000 of them. Expert analysis found 34 shaped tools among 167 pieces of 'mylonite'. It is clear that Barvas Machair has been occupied and used as a resource across several millennia.

CHAPTER 49

SEVENTEENTH CENTURY COINS AT BARVAS

One Saturday in 1979, a year after we had studied the Iron Age midden at Loch Mor Barvas, we were back on the Barvas machair. The digging of a sewerage trench had disturbed a strip of machair land, so we field-walked the area looking for potsherds, bones or other interesting fragments that might have been exposed.

Benjamin, then aged 9, rushed up in great excitement with an old copper coin which he had spotted. It was a little smaller than a 1p piece. Examining the worn surface, we soon distinguished 'LOYS XIII'. A strange find indeed. Back at home, gentle cleaning and examination under good lighting revealed further inscriptions, including the date – this French coin was minted in 1637. From photos, the National Museum identified it as a 'double tournois' of Louis XIII.

I also sent photos of each side of the coin to *Popular Archaeology*. My pictures appeared on the letters page of the June 1980 issue, with a comment from the magazine's coin expert, Tony Williams. He explained

Looking down at a small area of the Barvas machair. Field-walking requires a keen eye for fragments of bone, shell or pot while systematically traversing a grid pattern. Scale in cm.

that the well-worn coin could have been over one hundred years old when lost at Barvas. At that time, any copper coin might have circulated as change, especially on an island like Lewis, where buyer and seller generally knew and trusted one another. As a cautious archaeologist, he had no explanation to offer on how the coin first came to Lewis from France.

Rather remarkably, 'history repeated itself' almost exactly a year after the first find. Again, we were looking for pottery on the disturbed surface, again Benjamin was excited by the find of a small copper coin! It proved to be of similar date to the first, a Charles II Scottish tuppence. We wondered what activity brought the owner of these coins to the Barvas machair, probably in the latter part of the 17th century.

The obverse and reverse of the French double tournois of 1637.

197

The obverse and reverse of the Scottish turner
of around 1660.

My photos again appeared in *Popular Archaeology* and their expert
again had a comment –

*'This coin is a Scottish 'turner' or 'bodle' – twopence Scottish, minted in
the name of Charles II shortly after the Restoration in 1660. At the time,
an English shilling was worth twelve Scottish shillings and therefore
this little coin should have been valued at a sixth of a penny south of the
border. Like the French coin reported previously this one probably did
duty as a farthing. ...., judging by the amount of wear, it seems to
have passed through a good many hands before it was lost. It seems
improbable that anyone would take the trouble to bury the equivalent of
two farthings; the loss of a purse is more likely. If it was a small cloth
bag, all traces of it would have vanished by now, leaving only the contents.
A few more coppers may come to light if searches continue.'*

To continue searching, we borrowed a metal detector, only prepared to use
such equipment on land that we knew to be already disturbed. We obtained
permission to use it on the machair, both from the Factor of the Barvas
Estate and from the Clerk of the local Grazings Committee. We gave an
undertaking that we would deposit any further finds in the Lewis Museum
in Stornoway. Then we spent a damp Saturday afternoon searching over
the disturbed area of land where the two coins had been found.

Apart from the usual rusty nails and tin lids, which I understand are the bane of every detectorist, we found three coins – a half-penny from 1971, a penny from 1970 and a tenpence from 1971. This would barely have covered postage on our letters to the Factor! We returned the metal detector to its owner … and wondered if we were honour-bound solemnly to deposit the three coins in the local museum!

Ben, now in his 50s, is surprised that references to his finds still turn up in the archaeological literature.

CHAPTER 50

CUPMARKS ON NORTH UIST AND HARRIS

A Walk on North Uist

It was a fine day on North Uist in October 1979. The harvest was in full swing on the extensive tracts of machair. The tide retreating across the sands left a sparkling white expanse. At Sollas the experienced can drive for miles on the firm sands at low tide, providing the easiest route to the machair fields. Being wary, we chose to park where the track leaves dry land and to walk along the sands. It was an idyllic day of sun and silence, broken only by the twittering of wading birds far out on the tideline and the distant drone of tractors at the harvest.

Far out on the tongue of machair land lies Udal, which had been a thriving community in Bronze Age times, during the Norse settlement, indeed right up to the Clearances – but now a sand heap, an archaeological tell, a Hebridean many-layered Troy. Iain Crawford and his ever-changing international team of helpers had worked here for fifteen or more seasons.

199

Our guide to the current dig told us that they practised 'total excavation', a necessary technique in layered sites, in which every stone and feature is mapped and then removed. Nothing is left to see at the site, but a tremendous amount is added to our knowledge of past ways of life. We were told that, should we speak to Crawford himself, it would be tactful not to mention Troy!

We walked on to our second objective, Aird a' Mhorain (headland of the bent-grass), a small rocky sea cliff set among the sand hills. A flat vertical rock face about 2-3 metres high has a cross carved on it, recorded by Dr Callender for the RCAHMS in 1914. There is a freshwater spring near the base of the rock, called the Well of the Cross, but it is difficult to find, as high tides move pebbles over it. Nearby, flat on the shore, surrounded by and partly covered by pebbles, are rocks bearing cup-marks. The cross was probably a later addition, a Christianisation of a site thought associated with pagan beliefs.

Callender also recorded a pair of rocks with about 20 cup-marks. One has the marks arranged in line along the ridge of the rock. A few metres away among the pebbles, we found a third rock, about a metre by half a metre, bearing 40 cup marks of various sizes. As far as we knew, this rock was not previously recorded.

Southern Scotland, Brittany and Ireland

On the mainland in the summer of 1982, I visited some spectacular rock art sites, guided by Ronald Morris's book 'The Prehistoric Rock Art of Argyll'. At Achnabreck, deep in a forestry plantation, I located a roughly level sheet of rock, densely covered with carved cups, rings and spirals, the patterns in the rock showing up with particular clarity in low evening lighting.

Really sophisticated prehistoric rock art may be seen at Gavrinis in Brittany (chapter 56) and at Knowth in the Boyne Valley, not far from Dublin. Many fine drawings of the numerous decorated megaliths at Knowth appear in Martin Brennan's 'The Stars and the Stones', a book that was a pleasure to review for the Gazette. Incidentally, it inspired in me a wish to visit the monuments in the Boyne Valley, which I eventually achieved in 2018.

Rocks in southern Scotland have less complex art, the most detailed being the shapes of Bronze Age axeheads. However, Morris found that the commonest type of carving is the simple cup mark.

Why Make Cupmarks?

Cup-marks, although classed as rock art, are not especially artistic. Each mark is a man-made hollow in the rock-surface, often of a size that would hold a tennis-ball. It is common for thirty or more cups to occur on a single rock, which was generally almost level and an outcrop of bedrock rather than a loose boulder. The carvings must have taken considerable effort to create, especially in a rock as hard as gneiss.

The reason why prehistoric Man made cup marks on rocks remains a mystery. Morris collected up to 150 ideas, ranging from the extremely fanciful to the reasonably plausible. To some writers, cup marks have been sun-symbols, to others they are tally marks, places to grind herbs or leave offerings, or maps of star constellations.

Morris Visits Harris

When Ronald Morris and his wife visited Lewis and Harris in 1983, we were able to show them the first piece of rock art known on the island. First shown to us by George Macleod of Borve (Harris), the site is near the ruin of Dun Borve. We had recorded the discovery in *DES*.

On the sunny evening when we visited with Morris, the forty or so cupmarks on the almost level upper surface of a rock outcrop were showing up clearly. Our expert visitor was very interested to see the site; its chief significance being that its discovery extended the distribution of rock art into a new area.

Aird A' Mhorain

Professor Thom claimed that cup-marks were set out with a geometrical precision similar to that seen in the plans of stone circles; that there were circular and spiral patterns in their arrangements; and that dimensions were in his 'Megalithic Inches' (chapter 46).

We studied an enlarged photo of the cup marks at Aird a' Mhorain, poring over it for hours with tracing paper and coloured pens to see if we could match Thom's geometry. Inevitably, with 40 closely packed 'cups', various patterns could be traced but none were convincing. Like Thom himself, we returned to our main research interest – the megaliths.

Scottish Rock Art Project

Since 2017, this HES scheme has recorded many sites across the country. Its online database includes 37 sites in the Western Isles, nearly half of them on North Uist.

CHAPTER 51

BOG BUTTER IN THE PEAT BANK

In 1983, less than a week after the Dalmore site was finally back-filled, we received a phone call which presented us with a new archaeological puzzle. William Mackenzie of High Borve (Lewis) had found a hard ball in his peat, larger than a football and apparently composed of suet. We asked if the fat was in a pottery or wood container — *"No, it's just a ball and there is a second one still embedded in the peat"*.

So, on the following Saturday, we drove to High Borve and out to the peat banks. Mr Mackenzie had carefully left the ball in place, about two feet down from the turf, standing on a 'buttress' of uncut peat. The ball looked very much like a giant turnip! Where a slice had been taken off with the tarasgeir, the cut was white and suety in appearance and smell. A second ball had been left in place, its edge just visible in the peat face due to be cut the following year.

Mr Mackenzie described how he had been cutting a short length of bank on his own, to check the quality of the peat. When he first hit the ball, he was very alarmed. The white ball, covered with a thin layer of fibrous peat, gave the impression of a human skull with matted hair! However, in clearing the peat around it, he discovered that it was full of fat.

We had heard of 'bog butter' being found in peat, but were not too sure of its origin. When people spent their summers at the shielings with their cows, did they make large quantities of butter and store it in a hole in the peat to preserve it?

The fat at High Borve certainly no longer looked or smelled like butter, more like white suet. But it contained little flecks of clearer yellow fat and the odd hair. Margaret cleaned the peat face with a trowel to prepare an archaeological section. Our hope was that the edges of a pit, dug to bury the balls, would show up on the cleaned peat face. However, the only colour differences visible in the peat ran as horizontal bands.

Margaret's first view of the bog butter, with its finder William Mackenzie.

When the ball was lifted out, thin skin could be seen, some attached to the ball and some to the underlying peat. Both the ball, and the slice of peat carrying the pieces of skin, were sealed into polythene bags to prevent drying out – and temporarily stored in Mr Mackenzie's freezer!

The appearance of the skin is similar to the skin of a new potato, very thin, brown and fragile. Taking a small piece to my school Biology Lab, I examined it through a microscope, and could see blood vessels and a few hairs. It seemed probable that the skin was the remains of a leather bag that had enclosed the ball.

I looked up records of previous similar discoveries. In 1931, Hugh Mackay found bog butter while cutting peats near Kilmaluag on Skye. Amazingly, the wooden keg in which it had been buried was also preserved; it was 21 inches high and had been carved from a solid birch trunk over 15 inches in diameter. It had lugs and holes for carrying and for fixing a lid in place, a well-made and probably valuable item. The fat was described as white and cheesy with a smell and taste like that of rancid butter … no-one involved in the Borve find had felt inclined to taste the fat!

Hairs found within the fat from Skye were examined at Aberdeen University. Most proved to be from Highland cattle, but there was also a horse hair, a dog hair and several human hairs, both light and dark.

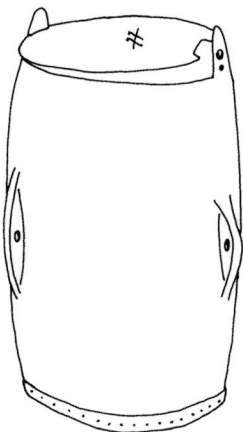

Wooden butter keg found in the peat in Skye in 1931. Redrawn from Ritchie, 1940.

Professor James Ritchie commented that the hairs suggested *'the domestic atmosphere of a farmyard, in keeping with the relics of blonde and auburn dairymaids'*. (!)

Local informants told us of a large earthenware pot of fat, found in Uig about 60 years ago. In locations as far apart as the Faroe Islands, Morocco and Kashmir, the practice of burying butter has been described, not just to preserve it, but to produce a locally enjoyed flavour.

I telephoned the National Museum of Antiquities about the new Borve find and was put in touch with David Caldwell, an archaeologist whose specialism was the period AD 1100-1750. (My notes on the Benbecula plaque, chapter 30, are based on his paper). Dr Caldwell was very excited about the find. A number of samples of bog butter had been taken to the NMA over the years, but there had been no recent analyses. And the ball that we had left in the bank at High Borve presented the first opportunity for a sample of bog butter to be collected under archaeologically-controlled conditions.

So, Dr Caldwell arrived on the *Suilven*, equipped for his mini-excavation. We introduced him to Mr Mackenzie, and he examined the first ball that we had lifted. Then we all went out to the peat bank, where we again cleaned the peat face for David to make a section drawing showing the position of the untouched ball.

Using the same method as that used at Leobag (chapter 41) a sample peat column was taken, intended for pollen analysis and radiocarbon dating in the National Museum laboratories. The second fat-ball was carefully removed, with a layer of peat still around it, preserving leather bag or other container. It was immediately sprayed with a fungicide and transferred to a large polythene box, also to be taken to the laboratories.

Forty years on, sadly I have managed to track down only two pieces of information from the lab studies. The thin skin and fibrous vegetable matter surrounding the balls was identified as animal gut or bladders and straw. A radiocarbon date for one of the balls suggests its deposition in the late 11th or early 12th century.

CHAPTER 52

FINDS OF HAZELNUTS
AND A TOY BOAT

When I was handed a small polythene bag containing seven small round objects, my first thought was: *'Why am I being given a bag of sheep's droppings?'*. In fact, the objects were hazelnuts, not commonly found on Lewis today — but these came from beneath the peat. As we have seen, parts of Lewis were more wooded in the distant past, with hazel and birch the commonest trees.

In the following weeks, as the nuts dried out slowly in a polythene bag, they lost their peaty colour and looked more like fresh brown nuts. Opening one of them, I found the kernel in a very shrivelled condition.

One morning in February 1983 at the Nicolson Institute, my colleague Tom Clark showed me a wooden item that he had found in Sheshader, when digging a hole to bury a dead sheep. It was the nicely-shaped solid hull of a model boat, about 18 inches long. Two depressions on the 'deck' must have been sockets for masts.

Tom showed it to Trevor Cowie, who sent to the National Maritime Museum at Greenwich. They described it as a *'post-medieval model of a fore-and-aft rigged vessel, probably a fishing boat'*. We can imagine a fond father carving the block of wood a few centuries ago, before fitting it with masts and sails. Perhaps he was creating a replica of his own fishing vessel, as a gift for his small son or daughter.

The boat remains in Tom's possession and from time to time graces local exhibitions.

CHAPTER 53

A VISIT TO THE ISLE OF ENSAY

On St Moluag's Day, June 25th 1983, a landing craft, more used to transporting sheep between the islands of the Sound of Harris, left Leverburgh with an equally packed cargo of Episcopalians!

This was the annual 'pilgrimage' by the congregation of St Peter's in Stornoway, and friends, to the restored chapel of Christ Church on the uninhabited island of Ensay. That it occurred on this particular day that year seemed quite appropriate, as the other early chapel used by this congregation, at Eoropie, Ness is dedicated to the Celtic saint, Moluag (chapter 37).

It is clear that Ensay was inhabited in the past; both from the appearance of once-cultivated strip fields, and from written records. For instance, Martin Martin wrote this of Ensay in 1703:

'Between Bernera and the main island of Harris, lies the island of Ensay, which is above two miles in circumference and for the most part arable ground, which is fruitful in Corn and Grass; there is an old Chapel here for the use of the natives; and there was lately discovered a Grave in the west of the island, in which was found a pair of Scales made of Brass, and a little Hammer, both of which were finely polished.'

The sand dunes on the west coast, subject to continual erosion from Atlantic gales, are littered with shells, bones and pieces of pottery. The potsherds are of indeterminate age, as most are not decorated, and as methods of manufacture in parts of the Western Isles did not change appreciably between prehistoric pots and those of the early 20th century.

From 1966, Professor of Anatomy Albert Miles had regularly visited Ensay to collect bones for study, seeing them as a convenient source of anatomical data. In 1971, erosion exposed walls and gables of a previously unknown chapel, earlier than Christ Church. As a result, he realised that he needed to take an archaeological approach. He published results of his excavations of the eroded burial ground in 1989. There were over 400 individual burials, dating from the 16th to the 19th centuries. Much later, in 2012, surveyors from RCAHMS recorded surviving walls of the chapel and burial ground.

While many of us visiting the island in 1983 strolled around the grassland and the eroding dunes, the main events of our visit were a short service in the chapel and a picnic near Ensay House. Rebuilt in the mid-1800s, it was long the home of the Stewart family. Till his death in 1979, the house was a welcome retreat for Dr John Davies from his tours of duty in Accra, Ghana. It was he who took the chapel in hand, improving on the restoration of 1910. Prior to that date, it had been used as a stable.

Christ Church, which may date from the 12th century, is tiny, only 23 feet by 12 feet with walls two-and-a-half feet thick. The congregation crowded in, standing room only, with dim light filtering through windows that are little more than slits. Rev. Emsley Nimmo suggested that the spirit of medieval Christianity had been recaptured, with a reminder that, in the Celtic church, monastic foundations on remote islands acted as 'powerhouses for prayer' for the whole church.

Only about 100 yards away stands a much more ancient reminder of human occupation on the island. On a hillock high above the chapel stands a single megalith, which seems to have acquired no other name than Ensay. Four feet eight inches in height but only eight inches thick, it is set at a considerable slant. Professor Thom considered that it might indicate midwinter sunrise over the Skye mountains, but this suggestion has never been followed up.

The prominent standing stone of the Isle of Ensay, overlooking the beach, Christ Church and Ensay House. Image © Marc Calhoun

An alternative theory to the astronomical is that prominent single stones were waymarkers, and this may also apply to Clach Mhic Leòid on Harris and to other solitary megaliths on Uist coasts. Certainly, as our well-laden 'sheep transporter' headed back to Leverburgh, the standing stone was clear on the skyline, perhaps having been intended to mark a good landing place on a sandy bay.

CHAPTER 54

SPREADING THE WORD

We were always concerned to make our researches available to other archaeologists, and where possible to the public, in person, in publications and on radio.

'Callanish - the Documentary Record'

In our extensive early research we examined all known plans and illustrations of the Callanish Stones, as well as early texts which we had tracked down. We made a full analysis of each document for accuracy and for plagiarism. We prepared a comprehensive report in the form of pasted-up pages with our analyses alongside the originals.

We photocopied each page and deposited spiral-bound volumes in Stornoway library and in Edinburgh archives, with copies going to others in the field. 'Callanish, the Documentary Record' was issued in 1979. Two years later we prepared a second report in the same format, 'CDR 2 – the Minor Sites'.

However, we hoped to convert our specialist report into a richly illustrated book with popular appeal. At Findhorn Publications, our editor, Marianna Lines, did extensive work on it before it was taken over by Canongate Press in Edinburgh. They issued an Advance Information Sheet for 'Callanish, Stonehenge of the Hebrides', which would have been our comprehensive tome, perhaps even a coffee table book.

Aubrey Burl provided a generous foreword, calling it a *'meticulous work of scholarship'*. It is deeply regrettable that the book's non-publication was a result of our marriage break-up.

In his 2016 excavation report, Patrick Ashmore wrote of our

Documentary Record: *'Their attempts to get this anthology raisonée republished in a more readily accessible format came to nothing, despite support from Aubrey Burl and others. In my view it still merits wider publication nearly thirty years after it was written, as the many references to it in this publication demonstrate.'*

In *DES*, Margaret, referring to our CDR volumes, had stated *'... in 2014 the work was transferred to a digital format, making the documentary knowledge widely available'*. An excellent idea – however, Historic Environment Scotland could find no record of this digital version in 2025.

Many years after my return to Hampshire, I discovered small books on Stonehenge and Avebury, *illustrated entirely by old engravings*. I contacted Wooden Books, who welcomed my offer to write another in the series. *'Callanish and Other Megalithic Sites of the Outer Hebrides'* contains reproductions of the most informative of the old plans and illustrations.

Our Other Books

After the initial success of *'The Standing Stones of Callanish'* in 1977, we published mini-guides to Dun Carloway and to Eoropie Teampull as well as a report on our discovery of *'Achmore Stone Circle'*. We were able, with the help of a friend in Suffolk, at last to publish *'The Story of Kesgrave'*, a detailed history of the community where we had previously lived.

By 1984, our original 1977 guide book was well out of date due to new discoveries, so we replaced it with *'New Light on the Stones of Callanish'*. In addition, based on our joint researches, I compiled *'The Stones Around Callanish'* as a field guide to the 'minor sites'.

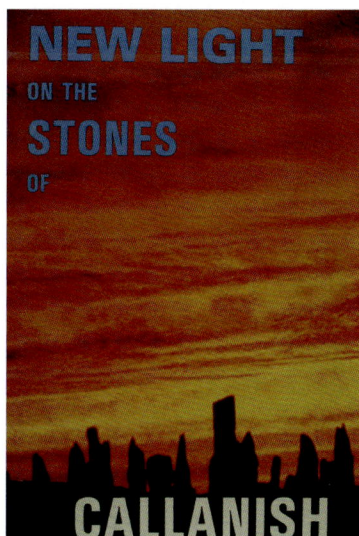

Newspapers and Magazines

My first archaeology article for the Stornoway Gazette appeared in January 1983. Intended as a weekly column, with other commitments it soon became less regular, but I wrote 63 articles over a two year period. Parts of 'The Lady and the General' (chapter 10) first appeared in *Eilean an Fhraoich*, an annual published by the *Gazette*.

Articles about our work appeared in several issues of *Current Archaeology* magazine (still published monthly) and in *Popular Archaeology*. I was on the committee that launched the journal *Hebridean Naturalist*, edited one issue, and published occasional notes in it.

Website and Youtube

It's probably a generational thing, but I have never made much effort to have an online presence. I have not kept my self-designed web-site up to date, but it does include a detailed bibliography of Callanish created in 2002; a full account of my return visit in 2006, hoping to see the southern moon skim; and a freely printable plan of the main Callanish site.

My lecture at Megalithomania in 2007 is still available on YouTube, though sadly audio-only. Also to be found on YouTube is my 2024 'Calanais Conversation' with the Prehistory Guys. There are other Calanais Conversations online, with interviews of others with specialist interests in the Stones.

In Person Talks and Tours

In Suffolk I had been a regular speaker at all sorts of societies, but there was less opportunity for this on Lewis. However, I gave colour slide presentations about Callanish from time to time, notably in preparation for my American trip (chapter 57).

When Craft Fairs were held in Stornoway Town Hall we generally had a stall. We displayed artefacts and often had interesting chats with visitors. But of course we also had our books and 'The Callanish Stones' T-shirts on sale.

An excavation volunteer at the Stones, wearing one of our Callanish Stones T-shirts.

We frequently gave tours of the Callanish Stones, often including some of the 'lesser' sites. We were booked for coach tours from Stornoway, including those from cruise ship visits, fairly rare events in those days. We once had an early morning phone call to meet a party of American tourists within the hour. We were twice booked by Swan Hellenic Cruises to lead all-day coach tours of Lewis.

For a Stones tour of an hour or so, the fee for one or both of us was £10.00 (equivalent to £55 today). But we also derived income from sales of our books – and visitors from the States were good tippers. One lady tipped us £15.00, which we tried to refuse, thinking she did not know the value, but she insisted.

Two particularly prestigious visits resulted from phone calls that came out of the blue. The first was from Aubrey Burl, whom we had met at conferences and with whom we remained in occasional contact. *My wife and I have just arrived in Stornoway, can we come and see you?* Of course, we dropped everything to give them a tour. It was a great opportunity to discuss our work and 'pick the brains' of a specialist.

The second call was from BBC Radio nan Eilean. *The BBC Chairman of Governors, George Howard, will be on the island on Friday – can you give him a tour of the Stones?'* Accompanied by William Carrocher of Radio Highland, he came straight to Achmore from the airport; we gave them tours of both Achmore and Callanish before they left, very impressed, for another appointment. I don't think we realised at the time that the Chairman was Lord Howard of Castle Howard!

All of our visitors*, whether professors of archaeology from Britain or America, or hippie-ish earth-energies enthusiasts, wanted to talk about our discoveries and to be given guided tours. Often they stayed for a convivial meal, sometimes contributing items from a planned picnic. Once we had a freezer, we stored emergency snacks – I well remember that de-frosted Rhum Babas always proved welcome.

Any new newsworthy discovery resulted in a call from journalist Bill Lucas. He interviewed me for the radio a number of times over the years and sent press items to papers based in Aberdeen or Edinburgh.

---

* Everyone was asked to sign our Visitors' Book. I would have been able to do some significant 'name-dropping' at this point if the book were still available!

PART 6

Elsewhere and Afterwards

———

CHAPTER 55

A METALLIC 'CALLANISH' IN GLASGOW

I had heard stories of a large modern sculpture, inspired by the Callanish Stones, on the campus of Strathclyde University in Glasgow. When I visited in 1982, I was surprised to find that it was a centrepiece of the University's campus. The sculpture is simply named 'Callanish', but is frequently nicknamed Steelhenge.

In a green landscaped area of lawns and trees, surrounded by the substantial architecture of a modern university, stand sixteen pillars, each 16 feet tall — similar in height to the tallest stone at the real Callanish. Each pillar is made from three tons of Corten steel, a material which is intended to weather to a rust-like colour without the further deterioration normal to rusty objects.

'Callanish' in Glasgow; four statuesque pillars stand in a close group at one end of the site. The shape has been compared to the iconic prow of a gondola, or more prosaically to washing-tongs – vintage laundry equipment!

My immediate reaction to the pillars was to stand within the group of four and to sight, past the single uprights and pairs nearby, to the distant pair on a mound. I wondered if any astronomical alignment had been incorporated into the design*. A Proctor on duty encouraged me in this belief, but it was probably wishful thinking on my part.

When the idea of a massive sculpture at Strathclyde was first discussed in 1971, the intention was to erect a major work of art, something that might prove to be the most important twentieth-century sculpture erected anywhere in the British Isles … maybe the Angel of the North or the Falkirk Kelpies took that title!

The sculptor Gerald Laing, born in Newcastle in 1936, worked in the urban confines of New York for six years, before establishing his rural

---

* When Sighthill Stone Circle was created a few years later and about a mile to the north of Strathclyde University, it was deliberately set up with astronomical alignments. These were maintained when it was moved and reconstructed on a new site in 2019.

studio in Conon Bridge, not far from Inverness. Affected by wilderness, weather and space in his new location, he wrote:

'... *the quiet authority of standing stones in the middle of fields, ploughed around by generations of farmers who did not understand them, yet did not destroy them, contains qualities also found in good art. So when in 1972 I was asked to make a sculpture for Strathclyde University, I thought of the great cruciform stone alignment on the Island of Lewis and let that describe for me the manner in which I approached the task.'*

Laing's Callanish pillars were in position by January 1974, but not officially 'unveiled' till June 1977. The sculpture continues to attract both support and dislike from those who see it. A member of university staff said that he was reminded of *'people in leisurely but studious conversation'*.

Laing hoped that his sculpture would restate Scotland's true values. He felt there was real danger of the nation surrendering its cultural identity, of losing the elements that once produced the Callanish Stones. Thus those who call it Steelhenge, by relating it to Stonehenge in Wiltshire, are missing Laing's point entirely.

Laing's design may be seen as a link between a modern technological university rediscovering spiritual values and the ancient skills of prehistory. By the construction of Callanish and other stone circles, ancient peoples demonstrated their aesthetic and spiritual awareness, their great mathematical skills, as well as their capacity for civil engineering and for social organisation.

Archaeologists might find it strange to imply an artistic intent on the part of the original builders of Callanish — although the site has an undoubted aesthetic effect in its correct context on the ridge above East Loch Roag. With this in mind, I tend to agree with the critic who said that Laing's 'Callanish' would be better placed on a wild windswept ridge, rather than standing on lush lawns and surrounded by educational edifices.

Perhaps the final word should go to the (nameless) university teacher who claimed it was *'splendid for human sacrifices, too'*!

CHAPTER 56

STONE ROWS AND CHAMBERED TOMBS

Carnac Stone Rows

We were so absorbed in our life on Lewis that we felt little desire to take holidays on the Continent. However, in the summer of 1983, on a sort of 'busman's holiday' from the Callanish megaliths, we spent a few days in Brittany and I based three *Gazette* articles on my experiences. Of the amazing Carnac stone rows, I wrote:

'Imagine the avenue at Callanish, nineteen stones in all, multiplied in both directions — ten stone rows wide, three-quarters of a mile long, with 1,099 stones in all. At the western end, the stones are huge, some of them larger than any stone at Callanish. The sizes are graduated along the rows, and at the eastern end knee-high boulders suffice to continue the lines.

Only a short distance beyond the end of these Le Menec rows, the Kermario alignments begin, tall massive stones at the western end, again grading down to the east.

Beyond this again are the Kerlescan rows, with a huge, almost square, 'stone circle' at its western end. Finally, Petit Menec is in wooded country, no stones much taller than a metre, and hardly ever visited by the tourists who drive the 'Circuit des Alignements'.'

Not far away, Le Grand Menhir Brisé (big broken megalith), now lying in four pieces, once stood nineteen metres high, surely the tallest stone of prehistory, visible for miles around. As at Callanish, one is left wondering at the inspiration behind these great monuments and at the skill required to erect them.

Chambered Tombs

I visited megalithic tombs in the Carnac area, comparing them with similar sites in the Western Isles. Barpa Langass on North Uist consists of a chamber, its sides and roof formed of great megaliths, covered by a huge mound of smaller stones. Back in the early 1970s, I carefully went inside with a torch, but it is considered unsafe to do so today.

Near Callanish, within the croftland of Breasclete, stand four contiguous upright stones known as Cnoc a' Phrionnsa, all that is left of a burial chamber. The position of the 'prince's hillock' (shown as 'Ph' on the plan in chapter 16) is such that it would have been a prominent feature of the landscape. As at other sites, any other slabs, as well as the smaller stones that once covered the chamber, were no doubt taken, over the centuries, as building material.

Unlike an Egyptian pyramid, built as the tomb of one powerful individual, many bodies were interred in such cairns, perhaps cleared out from time to time to make room for further generations.

An example of incised grooves forming intricate patterns on one of the megaliths lining the Gavrinis tomb in Brittany.

The most spectacular of the Carnac tombs is Cairn de Gavrinis. My visit required a scenic fifteen-minute boat trip in the Gulf of Morbihan. The exterior of the Gavrinis tomb has been extensively restored since then, but it is the interior that is of enormous interest. Twenty-nine huge slabs of stone form the walls and roof of a straight passage and a chamber. Incredibly, twenty-three of these megaliths are ornately decorated, a true masterpiece of Neolithic art.

I visited Tumulus de Kercado largely because Christine Maclagan (chapter 11) had compared it with Callanish, as both sites have a stone circle surrounding a chambered cairn. I discovered that the Kercado cairn was within the private grounds of a chateau, and open only for short periods. A few coins in an honesty box paid for a leaflet and the use of a key and a torch.

A walk in the woods led to a large and well-preserved burial mound, a single five-foot megalith standing at the centre of its roof. I found that Maclagan's comparison was just an on-paper similarity, as the Kercado cairn is huge, with the surrounding circle stones set at some distance, while the small Callanish cairn is within the circle.

The entrance was protected by a heavy wooden door. I wrote that *'even on a hot sunny day unlocking this door in the depths of a deserted wood, and entering the dank passage and chamber, was an eerie experience ... Royalist Britons are said to have hidden there during the Terror in 1792".* However, I was glad to have explored such an impressive and little-visited site. (Access, I understand, is somewhat easier today.)

CHAPTER 57

TAKING THE STORY OF CALLANISH TO THE USA

My five-week visit to the northeastern United States in the summer of 1984 was mostly spent as a tourist, including rubbernecking at New York skyscrapers and cycling around the Cape Cod National Seashore. I also visited some of the many excellent museums in Washington D.C., part of the famous Smithsonian Institution.

Smithsonian, Washington DC

However, my trip was also a 'lecture tour'. American delegates at the Oxford Symposium had been very keen for me to lecture on Callanish in the USA. The most prestigious of these invitations was to address the Smithsonian's Resident Associate Program.

I had prepared a new lecture, *'The Stonehenge of the Hebrides'*, including all of our latest research. I had given it a 'trial run' for several audiences in Stornoway in June. When setting up in the lecture theatre of the National Museum of Natural History in Washington, I was amazed – and a little alarmed – to be told that the audience would number *four hundred and fifty*.

I was also somewhat taken aback to learn that Professor Gerald Hawkins (chapter 9) would be in the audience. I met him briefly before my talk and was pleased to give him one of the very first copies of our new book *'New Light on the Stones of Callanish'*.

Sitting in the front row, during the introduction, my hands were sweating. On stage, I launched into my talk. Early on I showed a slide with an upside-down map of the British Isles, locating Callanish, as it were, at the centre of things. This amused my audience and any remaining nerves dissipated.

I was reliant on the professionalism of the projectionist in the booth at the back of the large lecture theatre. We had unloaded all of the slides from my magazines into his and I used two remotes for the side-by-side images on two screens. (For my other talks, I carried two projectors with me, housed in a wooden box, with a leather carry-strap, which I had constructed to the *exact dimensions then permitted* under a British Airways seat!)

Meeting people after the talk, I received a very positive response. I later learnt that some members of the audience had been inspired to visit Callanish, booking cruises to the British Isles. One young lady told me she would pass on my remarks to her father, who was responsible for a diorama of Stonehenge in the Smithsonian historical museum. I had cheekily slipped into my talk a comment that the display showed the sun positioned in a part of the sky where it could never be seen.

Following my talk, I was interviewed for Radio Smithsonian. As part of the interview, I gave this off-the-cuff explanation:

'I don't think there's any difficulty in saying that a stone circle was a means of watching the position of the Moon; the stone circle was a community centre; the stone circle was a temple; the stone circle was a place for trading; the stone circle would have held ceremonies for the funerals. I think all of these things could have taken place in the same setup.'

Harvard University

I also had an invitation from Owen Gingerich to an afternoon meeting of the Harvard Astronomical Society. At this second prestigious venue, my lecture was again much appreciated; one member favourably described my talk as *'totally unlike our usual colloquia'*.

New England, Societies and Megaliths

I also visited amateur archaeology societies at Woodstock, Vermont and at Stockbridge, Massachusetts. At my fifth venue in Groton, Connecticut, the society's attendance records were broken. Meeting enthusiastic members of each society on days following my presentations, they took me for walks in local woodlands to show me remarkable, but enigmatic, groups of archaeological sites.

Individual standing stones, like the megaliths of Britain, are notoriously difficult to date. Members of the Vermont society claimed that one in particular, almost six feet tall, was ancient. It was reputed to have the sort of mystical properties attributed by some to British megaliths. The official viewpoint is that this stone was a colonial gatepost, if unnecessarily tall.

I was also shown several megalithic chambers, of which there are many in New England. One near South Woodstock is especially impressive. Covered with a mound of earth, the internal walls are formed of neat dry-stone walling, while the roof is made of huge stone slabs lying across

Early Sites Research Society
presents

THE STONEHENGE OF THE HEBRIDES

an Illustrated Slide Lecture by
GERALD PONTING

of Stornaway, Isle of Lewis, Scotland,—following his recent lecture at the Smithsonian Institute.

The Standing Stones of Callendish, on the Isle of Lewis in Scotland's Outer Hebrides, are remote and little known. In the past they were believed to be a "council of petrified giants" or a "druid temple." Recent studies interpret the site as an observatory, part of a great megalithic complex. Gerald Ponting tells the full story of Callandish with superb color slides, personal anecdotes, and specially recorded music.

Tuesday Evening, July 24, 1984 at 7:30 P.M.
at the Woodstock Vermont Historical Society
Elm Street, Woodstock, Vermont
(entrance to the hall is in the rear of the building)

Admission $2.00   *Refreshments*

For more information contact
EARLY SITES RESEARCH SOCIETY, LONG HILL, ROWLEY, MA 01969 617-948-2410

Poster issued by Woodstock Vermont Historical Society for my lecture in July 1984.

the width. If found in Britain, no one would doubt that it was a prehistoric burial chamber. What is more, the entrance faces midwinter sunrise.

The official view of all the underground chambers was that they were root cellars. Certainly, colonial farmers stored root vegetables underground over the winter. Certainly, smaller chambers were deliberately built for this purpose. Certainly, some of the larger chambers were used in this way – but were the farmers re-using ancient structures that were conveniently nearby? Personally, I find it difficult to imagine a colonial farming family, scraping a living from the soil, moving a dozen Callanish-circle-sized megaliths, just to form the roof of a root cellar!

Some of the amateurs believe that the builders of these chambers were prehistoric European groups who had settled in America, long before Columbus, long before Viking explorers. Professional archaeologists dismiss the structures as colonial and therefore of no interest. They are more concerned with unearthing material records of Native Americans tribes – with no written records, technically they were prehistoric cultures.

With such differing attitudes between professional and amateur archae-ologists in New England at that time, my audiences envied the close cooperation with professionals which we enjoyed as amateurs in Scotland.

CHAPTER 58

LEAVING LEWIS WITH REGRETS

Margaret and I separated in 1983 and I lived in Stornoway for a year before I regretfully decided to leave the islands and return to southern England. In my *Gazette* column, *On Leaving Lewis*, I wondered if my life would take a different turn, after my involvement with nature conser-vation in Suffolk and archaeology on Lewis. I wrote, *Although I am returning to my native Hampshire, Lewis will always feel like a second home to me*. I anticipated frequent re-visits, but in fact I returned just three times over the past forty years.

I wrote of the things I would miss about Lewis – *'my colleagues and pupils at The Nicolson Institute ... the compactness of Stornoway – the conveni-ence with which you can do all your business and shopping in such a small area .... the openness of the moorland scenery, the importance of sky, weather, sun, moon and stars ... I'll even miss the wind! ... the many, many islanders (both natives and incomers) whom I have had the pleasure to know and to converse with over the years ... I am going to judge other ways of life, other attitudes, against Lewis – and find them wanting.'*

Geriatrix Pontifex

At a party for Nicolson Institute staff who were leaving, myself included, a comic song was sung to the tune of 'She Stood on the Bridge at Midnight'.

Finding a hand-written song-sheet among my papers, I loved the lampoon based on my megalithic interests! These are the two relevant verses:

Over by the Stones at midnight
Waiting for the equinox
Stood the High Priest of the Druids –
Geriatrix Pontifex.

Pickford's man received a letter
From the Isle of lateral shifts –
"Please remove to South of England
Thirty-seven megaliths!"

It's amazing that the erroneous connection of Druids with stone circles, based on the 18th-century writings of William Stukeley, is still stuck in the public consciousness. The Druids were an Iron Age priesthood, active around a thousand years after stone circles were in use.

CHAPTER 59

MOON AT ITS FURTHEST SOUTH IN 2006

One of my rare return visits to Callanish was timed for the most southerly path of the full moon. As a paper exercise in 1980, we had visualised the moon 'skimming' the horizon and setting between the circle stones as seen from the north of the Callanish site; and suggested that the alignment of the avenue with this event was deliberate.

Having missed the opportunity of seeing this rare event in 1987, I had been determined to be there for the next occurrence. While the moon reached its *absolute* furthest south on a single date, September 29th 2006, it would skim almost as low in the sky at four-weekly intervals for several months on either side of this date. I picked the night of June 11th/12th, as the moon would be full.

Before heading to Callanish at dusk, I had spent the afternoon of the 11th giving an impromptu guided tour of the Callanish sites to the American enthusiasts of Sheri Nakken's Earth Mysteries Tours. At Callanish VIII, a party of younger stones devotees gathered round as I talked to the American visitors; I found that they knew of me by reputation and wanted photos!

There were around 150 people at Callanish as the light slowly faded after sunset. Groups sat, walked and talked among the stones. 'Druidical' and 'pagan' costumes abounded. At eleven minutes after midnight, a glimmer of orange light appeared in the sky at the point where moonrise was anticipated. A number of joyous whoops arose from the waiting crowd, while the beat of drums began to rise to a climax, as if the rhythm would encourage the moon to rise.

Even now there was uncertainty – was there thin cloud on the horizon, above the prone figure of the Sleeping Beauty, which would prevent the moon's disc appearing? The excitement among the watchers was palpable as a thin crescent appeared, the upper limb of the full moon, just above the 'abdomen' of the sleeping figure.

The moonrise, with its unexpected musical accompaniment, was a magical and spine-tingling event. As it slowly rose, the moon slid along the body of the figure. At 12:20 a.m., the lower limb of the moon was just touching the 'breasts' of the figure. Two thin wisps of cloud across the moon's face only added to the atmosphere. (See photograph in chapter 19).

My hope, above all, was that the sky would remain free of clouds and that I would be able to see the moon set within the stone circle. But I was not to be lucky enough to see that supreme moment. The moon disappeared into cloud about halfway across its transit and did not appear again. Better luck in 2025!

CHAPTER 60

A NEW LIFE IN HAMPSHIRE

In 1984, at the age of 44, I was back again living with my parents in the cottage where I was brought up. But within a couple of years, I had a new home and a new family. Teenaged Rebecca decided that she would rather live with her Dad in Hampshire than with her Mum on Lewis. I met Liz, also recently divorced, and when we married we became a household of five, with my daughter and her two sons ... and two cats. Since then, our four offspring have provided us with seven amazing grandchildren and two young great-grandsons.

Meanwhile, Margaret stayed on Lewis, married Ron Curtis and continued archaeological research. She gave much appreciated guided tours till well into her seventies. Following her death in 2022, The Times and the Guardian both published obituaries detailing her decades of dedication to Callanish. Few connected the concurrent news story about thirty cats which needed rehoming.

Our son Ben inherited Margaret's home near Callanish. He and his wife relocated to the house that he had first moved to at the age of five, intending a total renovation.

In Hampshire I taught Biology at a secondary school not far from my childhood home. After seven years I gratefully took early retirement from teaching, but stayed on for a while as part-time Archivist, writing a history of the school. Through the 1990s I enjoyed my occasional role as a Blue Badge Tourist Guide, leading walking tours in Salisbury or Winchester, taking coach excursions to the New Forest, and so on. Guiding American tourists at Stonehenge was always satisfying, and I sometimes booked out-of-hours access within the stone circle for individuals.

No longer directly involved in archaeology, I was an avid viewer of the TV adventures of *'Time Team'*. When, in 2002, they undertook an excavation of rich Saxon burials in my home village, I was permitted to be an on-site observer due to my local history interest.

I was approached by a publisher to write a *Visitors' Guide to the New Forest* and this went through several editions. But most of my writing was for self-published local history books, Chris Weir's original offer (chapter 12) continuing to influence my life. With Anthony Light as the chief researcher and with me as co-author, photographer and designer, we published seventeen titles, mostly on the town of Fordingbridge and the village of Breamore. I also wrote and published books on other local communities with other co-authors.

Following my Wooden Book on *'Callanish'*, I compiled three more books in the same series, on *'Ancient Earthworks of Wessex'*, on the origins of the names of *'British Wild Flowers'* and on the traditions of the *'New Forest'*.

Through my years of teaching, I had another 'side hustle' as well as writing – slide presentations to local societies on subjects including wild flowers and local history. I expanded these activities on retirement, with digital images replacing transparencies from 2008. Since Lockdown, as well as giving personal presentations, I offer my talks remotely thanks to speakernet.co.uk.

I base travel talks on our foreign holidays. Liz and I have enjoyed visiting numerous Greek islands; as well as fly-drives in New Zealand, in Ireland and in Iceland; and safaris in Zimbabwe and in South Africa. Cruises took us to national parks in Madagascar and (before regime change) to Roman ruins in Libya. On a visit to north Norway, I was thrilled to photograph the Northern Lights. Incidentally, while living on Lewis, really spectacular displays of the Aurora Borealis occurred from time to time; but in those pre-digital times, I made no attempt to photograph the colours in the sky.

I have produced several talks on stone circles, including that detailed in the following chapter. *'Visions of the Stones'* is a presentation on Stonehenge as it has been seen by artists over the centuries. *'Callanish, the Moon and the Sleeping Beauty'* has intrigued audiences in southern

England. I used the title *'Archaeological Adventures on the Isle of Lewis'* for a colour slide presentation to local historical and archaeological societies … and adapted it for this book.

CHAPTER 61

'GOING ROUND IN CIRCLES', A NATIONWIDE PROJECT

Back living on the mainland, I visited many other stone circles. In 1995 I spent a few days on Orkney, mainly to photograph Brodgar and Stenness. Having assembled many colour transparencies, I put together a presentation, starting at and returning to Stonehenge. I called it *'Going Round in Circles'* and showed it to over thirty different societies between 1996 and 2006.

I wrote and illustrated a 68-page booklet with the same title, which I made available to interested members of my audiences. The conclusions that I wrote in 1996 concerning stone circles in general still seem apposite today.

Archaeologists can often answer questions beginning with 'When…?', 'Where?', 'How…?,' and 'Who…?' – but can never answer, with certainty, questions beginning with 'Why…?'. It is in the very nature of investigations in prehistory, defined as the period before written records, that we can never be sure of motives. We can never hope to 'see into the mind' of prehistoric Man.

I like to use a comparison with modern religion. If remains of our civilisation were to be explored by archaeologists of the distant future, without access to our written records, how much could they find out about

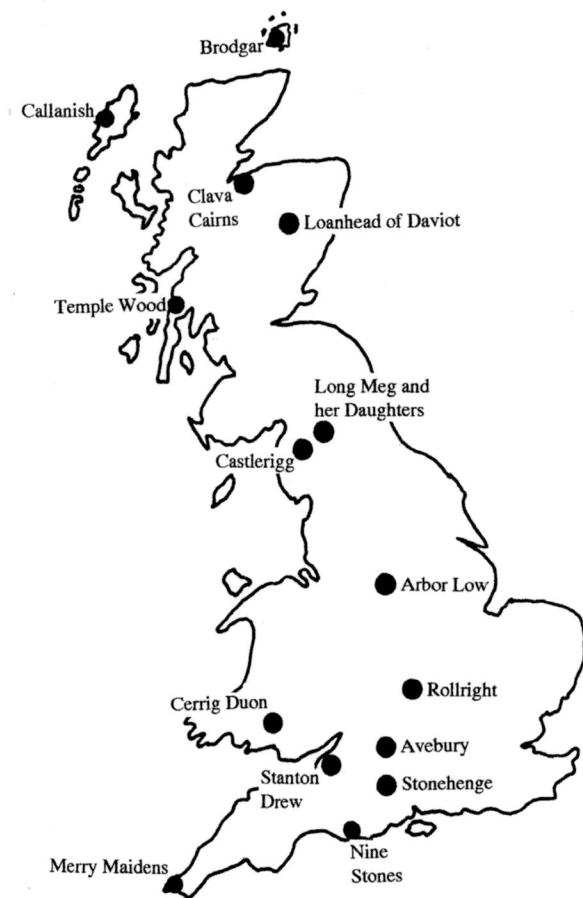

The stone circles throughout Great Britain which were featured in my 1990s colour slide presentation *'Going Round in Circles'*.

our way of life by studying churches ? In a church, they would find none of our domestic paraphernalia; for that they would need to excavate houses. Thus sites like Dalmore tell us more about the way of life than Callanish ever can.

Extending my comparison with churches, what would our future archaeologists make of the differences between, say, a Catholic Church, an Anglican church and a Presbyterian church ? It might be clear to them that the buildings were dedicated to 'ritual purposes' but they could never *be sure what the rituals were. Even less would they be able to distinguish the differences in ideology between the congregations.*

If we ask, 'were the circles temples, calendars, community centres, observatories, crematoria or status symbols for their tribes' the answer may be 'yes, all of these at the same time, without distinction'.

Stone circles probably had a multi-purpose use. The building of a circle was an important communal effort. The completed result formed a focus for all the important activities of the community — worship (perhaps of the Sun, of the Moon or of the Earth-Mother), dancing, trading, initiation ceremonies, marriages, funeral rites and so on.

The festivals of the agricultural year including planting and harvest were probably celebrated within the circle, as were the solar solstices and the infrequent extremes of the lunar cycle. The officiating 'priests' may have had astronomical knowledge handed down by oral tradition.

A stone circle may have been a 'combined temple and community centre' in one imposing site.

CHAPTER 62

CAMPAIGNING FOR ARCHAEOLOGY

In an article written in 1983, and quoted in chapter 43, we claimed to have increased archaeological awareness in the Western Isles, helped by newsworthy random finds. But my writings sometimes took on a specifically campaigning approach and I like to think that some more recent developments just may have been influenced by my writings.

Finds by the Public

I had encouraged local people to report ancient finds, even before I started to write regularly for the *Gazette*. The Shulishader axe might not have been carefully protected from drying out if the finders had not previously read my advice. I wonder if there are still items lingering around the islands, in the proverbial shoe-boxes, that should be declared as Treasure Trove and that would fascinate archaeologists.

Local Archaeological Expertise

Much information can be obtained by the rescue excavation of a site about to be destroyed. On the mainland the threat comes from new developments including road works, but in the islands, coastal erosion (chapter 48) is a bigger problem. The Central Excavation Unit of SDD (AM) took on such digs throughout Scotland, but some regions had their own local units.

In my *Gazette* column of March 5th 1983 I wrote: *'In the current financial climate* (sounds familiar?) *there seems little chance that Comhairle nan Eilean, responsible for an area rich in archaeological remains, could afford even a small professional Excavation Unit. How many interesting sites will be destroyed before the expertise is available to record these disappearing aspects of our heritage?'*

Today, the Western Isles has a council-employed archaeologist. The Archaeology Service, Arc-eolas nan Eilean, *'monitors archaeological sites and advises on the conservation and management of the archaeological resource … supports academic organisations, community groups and individuals who are involved in archaeological research … monitors all archaeological work happening … and aims to ensure that this is done to current standards and that **the results are made available to the public**. The service also curates the Historic Environment Record* [Clàr Àrainneachd Eachdraidheil nan Eilean Siar] *with over 13,000 sites included.'*

That quote is from the Comhairle's website, but with my added emphasis. In 2008, the Comhairle published three colourful popular guides to the archaeology of the islands – *'Ancient Lewis and Harris'*, *'Ancient Uists'* and *'Ancient Barra'*.

LandStory Lewis is a commercial archaeological service operated by freelance archaeologist Ian McHardy, author of *Contemplating Calanais*.

An Archaeology Museum

On the occasion of the Comhairle advertising a new post of Museum Curator, I devoted a Gazette article to *'A Plea for a Western Isles Antiquities Museum'*. I extolled the situation on Bute, where I had been taken to sites by a local expert, then visited the privately-run Bute Museum to see the finds from those sites. I deplored the fact that finds from the Western Isles might be stashed away in museum storerooms in Edinburgh, rather than being displayed locally.

I concluded my article: *'To stock an archaeological display at a Stornoway Museum would not be difficult. Given the security of a building and a professional curator in an established post, given display cases and other facilities, the story of island life through the Stone Age, Bronze Age and Iron Age into Viking times could be pieced together as a coherent story. Finds from important sites on the island would take their rightful place.*

And if Melina Mercouri can make so much fuss about getting the Elgin Marbles back to Greece, should our aim not be the return of the Uig Chessmen from London and Edinburgh?'

Museum nan Eilean opened in a secure purpose-built building at Lews Castle in 2016. Living in the south of England, I regret that I have not yet been able to visit, but its website suggests that archaeological finds do not form a major part of its displays.

The Stornoway museum has a sister establishment at Lionacleit on Benbecula, while there are several other museums around the islands. Local people and visitors now have plenty of opportunities to learn about the past.

My comment about the Elgin Marbles and the Uig Chessmen was somewhat tongue-in-cheek. However, the Scottish National Party has called for *all* of the Viking chess-pieces to be reunited on the islands.

At present six of the Chessmen are in Stornoway on permanent loan from the British Museum.

Visitor Numbers

In November 1983, I devoted an article to sites in my native Wessex, notably to problems at Stonehenge. I noted that Stonehenge received 531,000 visitors in a year. *'It would be interesting to know comparable figures for Callanish! They must be a tiny fraction of the Stonehenge numbers, but with no cash desk or turnstiles (thankfully) no figures are known for Callanish.'*

Calanais Visitor Centre was opened in 1995, with a major extension under construction in 2025. Visitor numbers in 2019 were estimated to be 150,000. With the opening of Stornoway's deep-water cruise terminal, this figure increased substantially, with an estimate of 300,000 by 2030.

Scheduling Minor Sites

In *'The Stones Around Callanish'* (1984) I wrote *'... there are many questions to be answered about the minor sites, which could be answered only by proper excavation. Archaeologists take note! ...... Were all the sites constructed at around the same time? ...... In the meantime, more of the sites should be scheduled as Ancient Monuments.'*

Callanish sites II, III, IV, V, VI, VII and XI were scheduled in the 1990s.

Excavations or other studies took place at Callanish VIII and VIIIA by the Curtises and at sites X and XI by the Virtual Reconstruction Project (chapter 16). Results are awaited for geophysical surveys at sites II, III and XI, also carried out by a team from the University of St Andrews.

Living History Museum

This is an edited excerpt from my *Stornoway Gazette* article of January 3rd 1985:

'While in the USA, I visited a living museum which attracts a large number of visitors. In a restored New England village, the way of life of around 1800 is presented by expert guides in period costume, demonstrating household, craft and farming skills to the visitors.

Think how interesting a preserved Hebridean blackhouse would be to tourists if it was the nucleus of a croft, operated using the methods of a hundred or more years ago. Costumed guides, local people who had re-learnt the old skills, could demonstrate them during the museum's opening hours. Obviously, when off-duty, they would return to the comforts of their modern dwellings! The scheme would attract more tourists and provide local employment. The museum could benefit from the sale of craft items.

As a final thought, an ideal site for the operation would be the old blackhouses at Garenin. They could be restored one by one and the museum opened gradually. Last occupied in 1974, they are sadly falling into disrepair despite their Conservation Area status.'

Comhairle nan Eilean set up the Garenin Trust in 1989. The blackhouses were restored, with modern amenities, and the village was opened by the Princess Royal in 2001. The Museum in one cottage represents life in a Lewis blackhouse in 1955, three years after the arrival of electricity. Four other cottages provide unique self-catering accommodation; there is also a seasonal café and shop.

World Heritage Status for Callanish?

In Britain, in Ireland and in Brittany, prehistoric sites have been given World Heritage status. The most prestigious, of course, includes both Stonehenge and Avebury in Wiltshire. In Ireland, 'Bend of the Boyne' includes the amazing tombs of Knowth and Newgrange. In Scotland, the 'Heart of Neolithic Orkney' includes Brodgar, Stenness, Maeshowe, Skara Brae and other sites.

UNESCO's 'Tentative List' of possible future World Heritage sites includes 'Sites Mégalithiques de Carnac' in Brittany and 'Zenith of Iron

Age Shetland' – the broch of Mousa and the settlements of Scatness and Jarlshof.

The whole area of Callanish deserves equal status with any of these. So, as my final piece of campaigning – when will the Scottish Parliament start the process to establish the *Calanais Ritual Landscape World Heritage Site?*

Acknowledgements and References

I would be impossible to thank all of those who assisted in some way with my studies in the 1970s and 1980s. Most will have received acknowledgement in earlier publications. However, I need to recognise that the interest of many island residents proved endlessly supportive in those years. The help of contacts in Edinburgh museums, libraries and archives was essential to our research and greatly appreciated.

Margaret and I benefitted from visits to Lewis by professional archaeologists, some of whom followed up on studies that we had started. They included John Barber, Sjoerd Bohncke, David Caldwell, Trevor Cowie, Joanna Close-Brooks, Mary Harman, Clive Ruggles and Niall Sharples. More recently, I have had helpful contacts with Trevor, Niall, David and Joanna in the preparation of this book. Torben Bjarke Ballin, lithics specialist, has provided useful information by email.

A special mention goes to Patrick Ashmore, the Ancient Monuments Inspector who had responsibility for the Callanish Stones, with whom we were in regular contact. His excavation report mentions his 'frequent discussions in person, by post and by telephone with the Pontings' which were often of mutual value.

Margaret's intelligence and dogged persistence were essential elements in most of the projects that I was involved with on Lewis. For our children, Benjamin and Rebecca (Benji and Becky, now in their 50s), family life was inextricably mixed, not just with sheep, goats, hens, peats and vegetables, but also with frequent visits to the Standing Stones, with potsherds and bones found on a beach, and with parental discussions about azimuths and flattened circles. They kept us grounded, found small ways to help, and benefitted from meeting all of the stones enthusiasts, with many different outlooks, who 'came to tea'.

Dr Alison Sheridan of National Museums Scotland and Urras nan Tursachan has been supportive of this book from my original concept. She has given valuable advice, corrected certain archaeological inaccuracies – and provided a generous Foreword.

Margaret Wilson of National Museums Scotland provided several photographs and permission to use them. Other permissions, acknowledged on individual images, were given by BBC Archives, British Museum, Mark Calhoun, Laurel Kallenbach of Colorado, Woodstock (Vermont) History Centre, Stornoway Gazette, Historic Environment Scotland, and Wooden Books. Images attributed to Margaret Curtis are now the copyright of our son.

My wife Elizabeth kept me supplied with coffee during the months that I was, in effect, reliving the years before I knew her. Several line drawings have benefitted from her artistic skills, and she was one of my efficient proof readers. Typos, errors and inconsistencies in my draft chapters were also tracked down by John Randall, Sylvia Harrison and Raymond Pratt, for which many thanks. I compiled chapters 9 and 26 following a useful suggestion from Raymond. Any errors which remain are of course my own.

My thanks to John Randall and Claudia Albrecht of the Islands Book Trust, Balallan, Isle of Lewis, for their support and encouragement throughout this project. Grateful thanks also to Michelle Walker at Palimpsest Book Production Ltd, Falkirk, Stirlingshire, for their thoughtful design and careful typesetting, which brought clarity and character to the pages. Appreciation as well to Gomer Press Ltd, Llandysul, Wales for their skill and attention to detail in producing the finished book.

If this book had a more academic approach I would have devoted many pages to a detailed bibliography. One that I prepared over 20 years ago may be consulted at https://www.megalithic.co.uk/callanish-bibliography/

ACKNOWLEDGEMENTS AND REFERENCES

Ian McHardy's *'Contemplating Calanais'*, published by Islands Book Trust in 2024, includes an up-to-date, detailed and very useful bibliography.

Further information on many of my topics may be found by judicious searching of the internet. For instance, entering the title of chapter 30 into a search engine gives immediate access to David Caldwell's original 1980 paper in the *Proceedings of the Society of Antiquaries of Scotland*.

In fact, all issues of the Proceedings from 1851 to the present day have been digitised, so that any paper of interest may be downloaded as a pdf from – https://journals.socantscot.org/index.php/psas/issue/archive

Similarly, all entries in *Discovery and Excavation in Scotland* are accessible from – https://www.archaeologyscotland.org.uk/about-us/publications /discovery-and-excavation-in-fscotland-des/

At the time of going to press, the Canmore website is being closed, to be replaced by the oddly-named 'trove.scot' online database. It should include details of all the archaeological sites mentioned in this book.

I hope that many of my readers will be inspired to have their own 'adventures', while discovering more of the ever-fascinating stories of earlier times, revealed by archaeologists throughout the islands of the Outer Hebrides.